REVELATIONS

Marge Mcfarlane

authorHOUSE®

AuthorHouse™ UK Ltd.
500 Avebury Boulevard
Central Milton Keynes, MK9 2BE
www.authorhouse.co.uk
Phone: 08001974150

First published by AuthorHouse 8/15/2011

ISBN: 978-1-4567-7908-5 (sc)
ISBN: 978-1-4567-7910-8 (hc)
ISBN: 978-1-4567-7909-2 (e)

HIS FIRST TEXT

"I am free now, at least for a few weeks," I thought to myself. This should have come as a relief but instead it came as a threat to me and placed me in a position where I was not only worried about my financial situation but also about my personal life. I had only officially left the British Forces, the Royal Navy (RN) in particular earlier in the year and had started at this medium sized mailing house company immediately afterwards. I was performing a mid-management role as a Production Administrator and my income was not as much as it was when I was in the Navy but at least it was paying the bills. I had a mortgage to pay along with other very significant responsibilities.

I woke up early, sick with worry at the thought of the increasing levels of unemployment and the planned cuts to benefits in the short run. The Conservatives, who had only just come to power, were making dramatic policy changes in order to shrink our deficit. The media was bombarded with all these changes that were about to come upon us and I am sure I was not the only one who was reminiscence of the Navy days or other fruitful source of employment, when my income was secure.

Though it was dark outside, I knew it was daybreak as I could hear the birds as usual which live just above my bedroom window in the roof. On this particular Wednesday morning they sounded sad and forlorn and the day was bleak and cold. On top of that, I was conscious of the big space in my double bed which I was contending with for over a year now and wondered if it was worth giving love another chance, for with all the notable men in my past, how is it that I am single today?

I turned over in bed, switched on my bedside lamp and looked at the clock, it was 0610. I was sad when the Personnel Manager and the Managing Director called me into the board room and informed me that I no longer had a job because the company was experiencing financial difficulties and so they were cutting back as a result. This came as no surprise to me though, because right throughout my short time with the company they were having problems purchasing their raw material, like toner and printing paper which they needed daily and they also had a large debt which they couldn't afford to repay. The family who created and owned the business was such a remarkable one, especially Martha, the mother of the Managing Director. It broke my heart to see what was happening to them. Because of what was obvious to me, that they were going through, I didn't feel as bad for myself when I was given the news.

I thought about my plan of action over breakfast which was simply egg and toast. I glanced once or twice at the television screen. I was aware that Countdown was on but I was not really registering what was going on. "I have to find a job." I told myself and I also must seize this opportunity to find an interest; someone I can talk to when I am lonely which is probably always these days, someone whom I can go out on dates with and hopefully things will develop into more, much more. I knew that if I was going to find someone it would have to be now because when I am out working I usually am so busy I have no time to even think of finding someone. I switched off the television and left the living room, swiftly threw myself in the computer cubicle, switched on the computer and sat in front of it. I loved the idea of having a private area to work on the computer.

I remember when I viewed this house and the seller Mrs. Kealey, who had put it up for sale only two weeks earlier told me all about how convenient this computer area was. I was not even sold on that idea but now that I've bought the house I realize how right she was. She was right about everything. She had said that the kitchen was a modern American style kitchen and had just been redone and was the selling point of the house, that all three bedrooms upstairs were massive and that both the front and back gardens were self-sustainable so I would save on gardening. What really grabbed me about this house when I came looking is that it was so clean, everything was spotless and in order. I felt like I wanted to move in right away. I remember how rainy and cold that day was in November 2008 when I had already viewed eleven properties and couldn't decide on putting in an offer for any of them because I just didn't feel at home enough in any of them to bother, except for this one. "I think you will like it here and I sure like the fact that you are from the Navy. I feel comfortable selling this house to you because I think it will be in good hands," she said with a broad smile across her face.

A lot of the sellers were friendly but I could see that she was being genuine and she was kind too. "Why don't you put in an offer?" She asked, smiling up at me as she got up from the beige sofa to walk me to the front door. "I will." I answered and politely stretched out my hand to her. "Thank you for inviting me to view your home on such short notice." I said, and as we shook hands I could see that though she looked about fifty, she was a petite woman with mousy brown hair and deep blue eyes. I had made the offer within five minutes of leaving even though I still had two properties left to look at which I was on my way to viewing but I knew this house was going to go fast and I figured that it would be better to put in an offer now and withdraw later than to lose out on the best property I had seen throughout my search for a home to buy.

I logged onto the internet now via Google and typed in directgov jobs. I searched through the not-so-long list of jobs available, which was very long until recently and for each one I was interested in I did a cover letter which I then attached to my Curriculum Vitae (CV) and sent off. I just kept going determinedly as I knew this was the best way to find a job and I had proven it before because this is how I found my last job, only, that time I opted to call the recruiting company first and then followed my usual routine of typing a cover letter and attaching it to my CV. This is a routine I knew I would have to follow daily if I wanted to be successful in finding a job. By about 1100 I was done.

I was tired but I knew I had no time to waste if I was ready to take on a partner, which I was. Right away I started thinking of the different ways to meet someone in this era of modern technology. I thought about the many months I had spent visiting churches of all different denominations, hoping to meet a potential partner but as far back as I can remember I never met anyone who was single. I hadn't had a chance to go out socialising much but I knew that had I had the time I still wouldn't have gone out alone because I hate going to the movies or out clubbing by myself.

Since it was clear I wasn't going to meet someone naturally, then I was left with no choice but to utilize a dating site which is the most popular source of finding a date these days. I wouldn't have explored this option normally but a very good friend of mine from university, Kelly, explored the same option eight years ago. Today, as a result, she is happily married for seven years and they just had a beautiful baby girl. I placed an ad in the newspaper; in the love2love column (most local newspapers have a love2love column). Love2love also has an internet link but I preferred using the print media. I can remember exactly what I had put down: I am an ambitious, beautiful, caring, sincere and honest 38 year old woman looking for an ambitious, handsome, sincere, tall and kind man for dating, relationship and possibly marriage. It was exactly one year since I had been divorced and I felt like I had my fair share of being alone. I hadn't been with a man for a year and a half. I was not used to this kind of lifestyle.

Rosie and Melissa were playing in the back garden next to the tall, white picket fence which was the only thing that separated them from the beautiful white-sand beach. There were times when their aunt Stacey would open the gate and they would rush towards the great blue body of water in their bathing suits with their buckets and shovels by their sides. There, they would spend the afternoon swimming in the shallow end of the sea and making sand castles in the cotton soft, pearly white sand. Their cousins, Asher and Katie were always by their sides sharing a joke or just having a laugh and competing with each other.

"Rosie, don't go any further!" Stacey would always shout as a warning to both pairs of girls to stay in the very shallow end of the water. Stacey knew too well that once Rosie was doing what was right then the other girls would follow suit as she was the eldest of the lot. As soon as the girls moved onto the sand Stacey would spread her towel next to them and put her shades on to protect her eyes from the glaring sunshine. She was very attractive, trim and petite with dark brown, back length hair. She was the youngest of her siblings and was doing very well for herself. She had graduated from university a few years earlier and was married to and partnering with Tom, an architect whom she met at university. They were in the business of constructing resorts in the tourist industry and though they started out small their business was growing off the Richter scale so she could afford to spend most afternoons with the children while she bask in the sun.

She had everything going for her but she was humble. Since she was a child she was never one to be boastful but was always very practical and level headed, as were most of her siblings. Rosie and Melissa looked out through the fence at the beach as they threw the big yellow ball at each other and they knew that they were going to miss it. They had become accustomed to going to the beach in the afternoon and spending time with their aunt, uncle and cousins but they knew that today was their last day in Montego Bay as their uncle Sheldon was on his way for them. The girls loved going on journeys though and were anxiously awaiting their uncle's arrival.

On Thursday I was up by the crack of dawn and did my job search straight after breakfast. By this time my appetite was declining because of my worries and I would have skipped breakfast if I didn't know better but I was fully aware of the consequences of missing meals; weakness in body and mind, exhaustion and stomach ulcers are only the beginning. Furthermore, I was trained by the Navy to always have my meals come low or high water so there was no options in the matter of meals, it just has to be done three times a day every day. Bearing this in mind I scuffed down my oatmeal, afraid that if I tried to eat anything else I would puke. My job search went smoothly and by 1100 I had sent out six applications for the posts of field researcher, production manager, quality controller, receptionist, office administrator and school teacher. I would have applied for more jobs were there more which commensurate with my qualification. One would have thought a degree majoring in Sociology would have afforded me more job options than those. The fact that enough jobs were not on the site to meet the high demand wasn't very motivating either. I just hoped that I would get lucky and get an interview at least. I wiped the sweat from my brows as my stomach sank from the prospect of not finding a job at all. This job site was the best one I knew of, the main one that was recommended by the Job Centre. Other sites like the job's mine and total jobs.com I tried occasionally but didn't feel that they were as reliable as directgov jobs.

I was sitting on the sofa now just staring at the television, Come Dine With Me was on and this dreadful looking woman with tacky clothes and too much make up was saying her main course would be sea bass and I thought to myself that if she dressed that way what could you expect of her cooking, would it be the same standards? I had only just finished that thought when I heard a text on my mobile phone. My phone was on vibrate for incoming texts and I jumped back to reality as the phone shifted from side to side on the glass, coffee table in front of me. I slowly picked it up and, as it was a touch screen phone, touched on the text with my thumb and it opened up to reveal that someone named Glen was introducing himself to me.

He was a 5'9" gym instructor who weighed 15 stones and lived in Hull. I marvelled at the speed at which this dating site worked and suddenly felt like my luck was changing and though he might not be the one for me at least things were beginning to happen. I could not get around the fact that though I was living in Greater Manchester I was being introduced to someone all the way in Hull. How was I going to date someone from such a long distance away? I decided though to make the best of it because at least it meant I would have someone to exchange pleasantries with, if he was that way inclined. I text him back describing myself as 5'7", attractive, weighing, 10 stones, who is smart, honest and sincere and lived in Greater Manchester. Right away he sent me his picture and asked me to send him mine but I felt that it was too early and asked him to allow me to do so at a later date. He didn't seem too pleased with my decision but went on to tell me more about himself. I knew that he and I wouldn't amount to much so I kept any information to him very limited and carried on texting him for the sake of having someone to communicate with. Glen text me all the time, even when he said he was at work. I probably was getting about thirty messages from him in twenty four hours. This went on for a few days and by the fourth day he started texting that he was horny and I knew it wouldn't be long now before I would stop texting him.

The second potential date was Harry who text me on the Friday. Because Glen was texting me too it might have been a bit tricky finding time for both of them but Glen was annoying me so I only responded to his text when I felt like it. Harry was 42, had 2 girls, was divorced, 6'2" tall and worked odd jobs for his father who own a number of apartment buildings. With him there was more of a chance because at least he lived in Greater Manchester. Sometimes he would sound so sad when he talked about the life he used to have and how he didn't know why it all changed. Sometimes in the evenings when I wouldn't hear from him for a while he would tell me later that he was putting his daughters to bed because he had them over at his apartment some nights. He seemed like a good father but I thought he was not really ready to move on and even worse, he wasn't confident enough. He would always text me whenever he was on break at work or whenever he wasn't doing anything. Sometimes in the mornings, while I did my job search, he would wait for me to text him and whenever I didn't he would complain later saying; it seemed I was busy texting other men.

I stopped texting him shortly after Monday too, not chiefly because of his attitude but because someone else text me at about 0330 on Monday to introduce himself and I felt instinctively that he was the one for me. There were other men introducing themselves to me but either from the first text or somewhere along the line I just lost interest in them and I really wasn't impressed by any of them anyway, that was until that first text came long before daybreak that faithful Monday morning and woke up my desires. I had gone to bed that night after my nightly shower and felt like I was no closer to finding a date. Though my bed was warm, I was too aware of its emptiness. It was a cold night but I had the heating on for the last three hours before bedtime. It was 2130 when I put on my floral print night gown and climbed into bed. I was communicating via text messaging with about six men by that time, including Glen and Harry, and I felt like they were all hopeless cases. I lay in bed with my mobile phone trying to get the message across to them all that it was bedtime and I was trying to go off to sleep.

Most of them got the message as soon as I text goodnight to their phones and they sent me a good night text in return but Harry ignored the words goodnight in my text and went on for about half hour after that and then it finally hit him that I was trying to get to sleep. It was much worst with Glen though because I don't think he realized that even if he didn't think he needed sleep for some strange reason, that he should still respect other people's need for sleep. I told him goodnight again about an hour after Harry said his goodnight and yet he still carried on as if it was the middle of the day. I was a bit furious by then and what was more upsetting is that he was doing this every night now since the first night we started texting each other. I was this close to telling him not to text me anymore but instead I checked the time on the clock on my bedside table. It was 0030. From upstairs in the master bedroom where I lay, I heard a car slowly squeaked by. A group of young people walked cheerfully past, singing songs of merriment shortly after and I wondered if they were returning or on their way to their night out. Minutes later I heard my phone vibrating and I knew it was Glen. I was so upset; I had to coax myself into relaxing in order to go to sleep. Again, deep in my sub-consciousness I could hear my phone vibrating but before I could react I was fast asleep again.

About 0330 I shifted and turned over in bed to face the windows at the front of the house. I was aware that something in the dark had awoken me but I wasn't quite sure what it was. Then it occurred to me that it must be my mobile vibrating again and I knew I had to tell Glen not to text me anymore. I really tried to avoid doing so but I felt I had to put my foot down now. I quickly glanced on my phone, read the first two texts, which as I expected were from Glen and just before I opened the third one I was overcome by sleepiness so I decided it would just have to wait until morning. To my surprise as I sat in front of the television after breakfast and read the text I realized it was not from Glen at all but instead it was a message from George introducing himself. He was 6'1", handsome, 16 stones, was an honest, charming, kind and gentle 39 year old man who drove a BMW and lived in Greater Manchester.

Instantaneously I felt a connection with him, which was a bit odd. I text him in reply with the same short description of myself I had sent to all the others I had been texting and he seemed genuinely happy to hear from me without mention of my delay in responding to his text. He sent me a picture of himself and I saw how desirable he was. My heart thanked him for being honest about his looks because so many of the other men who text me and said they were handsome, were nowhere near handsome as far as I could see. I suppose you can't knock them for thinking a lot of themselves anyway, nonetheless, beauty is in the eyes of the beholder. For a moment I just stared down at his picture, thinking about him and trying to answer so many unanswered questions.

From that moment on I had this strange feeling in the pit of my stomach that I had found what I was looking for. "I have found what I was looking for." This statement resonated a whole lifetime in my past within me. I could hear my sister, April, asking of Chris, "You have found what you were looking for, haven't you?" and I shyly answered "yes", ashamed of being placed on the spot in front of the one I loved. Chris was my first love and it hadn't been long since we had met. We, along with my sister and a handful of close friends were spending the weekend at the University House, up in the hills of the Blue Mountain in Jamaica. It was a very attractive house, which had all the appeal of a stately, luxurious hide-away.

On the Friday evening when we arrived we stopped the small mini-van in front of the large steel gates, the house was not in view but there were flowers everywhere and it was beautiful but that was only a slight indication of what was yet to come. We were warmly received by the caretaker and his wife and quickly given a tour of the premises. The house was a huge, old fashioned country cottage with all the allure of a palace. It was built from wood and was two stories high with a veranda and there were flowers all about this house and all around the grounds, the most beautiful and well cared for flowers you can ever imagine. My heart ached from the beauty of it all: the place, the company and of course the warm, golden sunshine.

George sent a text asking me for a picture and I sent it to him right away without hesitation for I knew I couldn't take him through all the usual checks and tests that women in our society today are usually taught to do as a part of our upbringing, whenever we meet someone we have interest in. He then thanked me for the picture and apologised for being forward, saying he would have waited but a picture tells so much and he was a bit anxious. I thought of all the books that I had acquired from church, my family and from book shops about dating and courting and I knew they were out the window. I knew I wasn't going to be playing by any rules written in any book with George. If hell should have its wicked way yet again and I should lose this man, a man whom I already felt so much for even though we hadn't yet met face to face, it wouldn't be because of a book. I found that instead of choosing carefully what I tell him, like I did with the others, I just went straight ahead and told him what he wanted to know whenever he asked any questions.

I remember one of my colleagues in the Navy, O'Neil, who met a girl on Face Book. She was living all the way in Austria and they text and talked to each other on the phone for about three months, at the end of which he flew all the way there to meet her and spent a few weeks of his holiday with her. In less than a year they were married and he had put in his notice to leave the Navy to live with her there. "How weird is he?" I used to ask myself when he confided in me how he felt about her and what his plans were. Now I could understand completely what he was going through. By the end of that Monday I was so thrilled with the thought of George texting me that I forgot my gloom. By the time I had my shower and snuggled up in bed I realized that I had forgotten to text the others though they were texting me all day.

From the moment I got that very first text from George, what little interest I had left in keeping up conversation via texting with the others was gone. I did not feel guilty about it. I just felt that the dating site had served its purpose. Even after that I kept getting introductory texts which I deleted and later sent STOP to customer services in order for them to stop sending me introductory texts. After saying goodnight to George at 2230 the night before, I slept soundly and woke up the next morning feeling sure of myself. I made egg, bacon, sausages and toast for breakfast and I welcomed the delicious smell of the food cooking on the cooker just as much as I welcomed it in my stomach.

I ate hungrily as I eagerly awaited his first text of the day. "It is going to be alright", I told myself. I did my job search and half way within it George text me saying good morning and that he didn't want to text too earlier because he was afraid that he would wake me up. I quickly told him

I was up by 0600 in the mornings and also briefly told him about my daily routine. What was touching about him was he; was saying "sorry" and "thank you" in all the right places. I wondered if it would be as wonderful to talk to him on the phone and I longed to hear his voice and thought of a loving, caring voice, especially at night, soothing me off to sleep.

It was three days now since we were texting each other non-stop and I was really longing to hear his voice by this time but I didn't want to be the one to instigate it. I wondered how he felt about me and if he was longing to hear my voice too. I knew there were a lot of things that were appealing about me, but, "my voice isn't one of them," I thought. I didn't think my voice was appealing, though I've had a lot of compliments to the contrary. I've been told that my voice was sultry and even caused arousal in my former lovers. I hoped it would have that same kind of effect on George.

On Wednesday my feelings for George had not changed and I went about my usual routine thinking about him in the back of my mind. By bedtime I was still wide awake and rightfully so because George was texting me constantly and I was loving it, I could tell that my extra gusto came from texting him. He told me he was a late sleeper that night and I decided I didn't mind staying up a bit later for his sake. Originally I was a late sleeper myself but when I joined the Navy I learned to accept and appreciate a hard day's work and a good night's rest in return; as long as it could be afforded. We text each other at length that night into the wee hours of the morning and that's when he asked me.

I remember how happy I was in my warm, cosy bed. I was smiling away at his last text. "Do you wear pyjamas to bed or night dresses?" he had asked. I replied, "Night dresses." And his response was, "I thought you were going to say pyjamas because you were in the Navy." Then his text went on to say, "I like the fact that you are military trained because you won't let anyone take advantage of you." I smiled to myself not knowing what to text back and I thought to myself. "So, he likes a strong woman, does he? So, I've found myself a real man?" When I failed to reply in the time I usually take he sent me a second text saying he was sorry for keeping me up that late but he would really love to have a talk with me on the phone the next evening as soon as he leaves work if that was alright with me. I froze for a while and he must have figured it out because he text me again saying he was hoping it was a 'yes' and he would text me in the morning.

OUR FIRST CONVERSATION

My mobile was ringing. The ring tone was ascending and each ring was compelling me more and more to answer it. I stared down at it. I had become a statue as my mouth became dry and my body numb from all feelings and emotions. This was the moment I had waited for all my life, and what other woman whether young or old didn't expect this moment to come at some point in her life whether it would actually be realized or not? This pushed me to remember a woman named Sarah I had known years before. She was a lecturer at the university where I worked at one point and attended lectures. It seemed everyone knew her story and I always felt such deep sympathy for her but no one including myself was ever bold enough to make reference of her experience to her face.

When she was younger and prior to her job as lecturer at the university, she was a beautiful young bride 'to be'. Her fiancé was a most, desirable bachelor and they were Christians in the church. One warm summer's day in June she proudly walked down the aisle on her father's arm to the tune of "here comes the bride" looking as beautiful as ever in her sassy bridal's gown, ready to repeat her vows. Meanwhile, all their specially chosen, extravagantly attired guests waited in anticipation. But so near yet so far away, for this man who seemed so faithful, sincere, trustworthy, kind, gentle and honest for the three years they dated prior to this special day, when he was asked if he takes this woman to be his lawfully wedded wife, he responded "No," after a long, painful hesitation.

Everyone sighed in disbelief, and then horror struck shortly after. He then faced the church and apologised saying he was sorry but he was in love with someone else. Then a young woman sitting among the guests approached the altar and he introduced her proudly, they then ran out of the church hand in hand. Anyone would have thought she was the bride. Unfortunately, what should have been the best day of Sarah's life turned out to be the worst day imaginable as she couldn't cope with the deception, the disappointment and rejection. She had a nervous break-down which took over her existence completely as she was never able to recover and move on with her personal life.

In retrospect, I too have had my share of disappointment years earlier when I lost my virginity to the man that I loved, Chris, a student at the university where I studied. I remember how very appealing he was; tall, dark and handsome. He had a solid structure, was very pleasant to talk to and was always quick to smile. I find that it was always hard for me to resist a man who had a pleasant mannerism, was amusing and who could smile easily. This I put down to my upbringing which was a bit strict as I was raised in a Christian environment, along with my eleven siblings. By dating men who were not quite as serious as my parental figures and mentors in my childhood I felt was an escape from my harsh reality. This brings to mind Freud and a quotation from his theorizing on 'Love-choice', which states: "Generally speaking, it is our past experience that prescribes what kind of attraction we will be most susceptible to. Specifically, the love-preference is formed in very early life in the relationship between the child and its parents. It is the family, so notoriously powerful in shaping personality, that designs the pattern of the erotic career, just as it blueprints so many other features of growth". The Love-Choice according to Freud, originally published 1957, www.oldandsold.com/articles09/sexual-emotion-46.shtml.

Chris was also a brilliant young man who majored in Economics but chanted politics so much that he could write a book about it any day. He was always on top of every aspect of his culture; it was all about the latest music, the latest dance, the most current clothes brands, the coolest styles and fashions and even the newest slangs. I think he loved me blindly as I loved him. We were young and innocent with our hormones running wild and even though we had the responsibility of placing our education as top priority we put nothing but the love we felt for each other first. We spent every moment together as long as we weren't hindered by any lectures or tutorials that couldn't be missed. It was as if we were joined at the hips. Whenever his paternal grandmother who lived next door to the university in Elleston Flats was away on her yearly trips to the United States for six months at a time she would leave him in charge and we would live there as man and wife.

It was during this period that I remember like it was yesterday, one fine weekend when the skies opened and showered down an endless body of rain on the island. We stayed locked down for those two and a half days and made wonderful, passionate love, all of thirty seven times. They were thirty-seven beautiful orgasms for the pair of us and at that rate, looking back, that was a very powerful relationship full of lust and love and I am glad that we survived it to tell the tale. When he finally got his dorm on Chancellor Hall, which is the most desirable hall for males on the campus. We lived in it like it was a luxury hotel. We went to all the university dances and discos. Those were magical years never to be forgotten. The first three years of our ten years together were glorious and free from any hurt or regrets at which time Chris proposed to me and I accepted with a big smile from ear to ear. I was happy for we had spent the last three years establishing our relationship and it was turning out to be what all our friends and relatives were expecting.

Unfortunately, the four years following our engagement were luke-warm which served as an obstacle which prevented us jumping our next hurdle which was meant to be our wedding. We found that as we were in our early twenties we started spending more time with others within our social group and less time by ourselves and because we had built a relationship which was focussed on being together by ourselves we were not accustomed to letting others in, so our relationship suffered and after the last three years of our ten years together we didn't even have a relationship that was worth salvaging. Chris had gone to England to do his masters degree in Financial Economics, as he was a mid management member of staff where he worked with the Jamaican government, a masters degree in this area would definitely pay off.

We were apart for fifteen months and even though he returned for a very short visit during spring break and I also visited him in England during that summer, there was no come back for us. It was as if someone had put a knife in our relationship and ended what Qupid himself had put his personal seal on ten years earlier.

The rain was thumping down on the roof top and Rosie and Melissa curled up next to each other on the sofa as they watched the water splashing heavily against the glass windows. It was like a typhoon but Sheldon and his wife Beth were now used to it, they knew that it would be over by nightfall. At times like these they would just curl up in each others arms and listen to the rain and the wind. They held each other hands as they watched the girls and were glad they were given the chance to play parents for the next few days because they had no children of their own yet and were happy just being with each other, just the two of them, for now.

Both he and his wife did their degree in Accounting. He studied at the prestigious Morehouse College in the USA and she at the University of the West Indies (UWI). They met when he visited the university bowl for his track and field training and they, both petite and very attractive couldn't keep their eyes off each other. Sheldon looked at Rosie and marvelled at how much she had grown. She was ten years old now and was the spitting image of her father. In fact, she had every likeness of her father and non to her mother. She was tall, he noted, and would probably be a model type in a few years. She was also pretty but not in the Style's family way. In the morning they would take the girls out for a walk along one of their popular trails to experience the fresh country air, and then they would take them to the fair later on.

I looked down at my mobile again. The ringing was even louder now. It was clear in my mind what I was looking for, someone who I could share my life with, a companion, a faithful one who I could always rely on, who would be there for me and with me every step of the way. Someone who would love and adore me and build a life with me, not someone who would prefer to watch me build it from a distance while they stay away from the heat of life's bitter struggles, where it is safe. I prayed a little prayer to myself, "Dear Lord, let it not be my ex-husband all over again".

My marriage to Roger, who is also a past student at the university which I attended was not always a living hell but it was hell often enough for me to plead forcefully and file for a divorce after five years of marriage. We got married after being friends for six years. It was not a passionate relationship, ours, we were mature and sensible and we knew what we wanted, or so we thought. My world wind of a relationship with Chris had ended for a while and I vowed to myself never to fall for someone so hard ever again. I longed for a practical and realistic relationship. Roger didn't have the characteristics that I usually look for in a partner. In fact, he was the exact opposite to what normally appealed to me.

He was a Christian in the church, a very strict individual who was never one to be impulsive or worry about brands, style, fashion or how he carried himself. He was very laid back in many respects and didn't care much what others thought of him. I think what I liked most about him back then was the fact that he was secure and also that nothing about him reminded me of Chris. I was too hurt by Chris and too determined in nature to take such a chance with love again. Roger and I met at the University Main Library. We were introduced to each other by Mrs. Green, a Librarian while working as Student Assistants. We were just casual friends for many years. Roger knew Chris and thought, like most people who knew us as a couple, that we would get back together one day. Now that I look back I think that was Roger's first interest in me.

Several years later when Chris and I were still not back together Roger started asking me on dates. Even at that time I think he was still just safe-guarding me for Chris. When Roger completed his master's degree in Accounting at the university and a few years later he unfortunately lost both his father and his paternal grand-mother who mothered him, as his mother had died when he was only very young, we began to get closer. Our reality was that we were not getting any younger and Roger felt that with the recent death of both of his parents he had a void in his life to be filled, for even though he had a step-mother, Lotty, whom his father had married after the early death of his biological mother and his three brothers, he didn't share a very close relationship with any of them. His eldest brother, Keith, was on his mother's side; Roger followed him two years later and was the first child within the marriage, then came Mark, who is also two years younger than Roger and several years later Alan was born.

One night Roger and I spoke at length, I was a member of the Royal Navy at the time and that weekend I was at Temeraire in Portsmouth playing sports for the Navy with a group of colleagues that I met during Naval training the year before in 2003. I was particularly lonely that weekend and I felt like my social life was dead and buried. It was very late on the Saturday night when we spoke at length which we always did on a daily basis from my very first day in the Navy. One thing about Roger, you could never be disappointed with him as long as it had anything to do with 'time'. He called every day as promised, stayed on the phone until I was happy and always called on time which is one thing I was impressed with in the beginning. I guess he wanted to be there for me because he knew that being in the Navy can be a bit challenging at times.

At the end of our conversation that night I had a warm feeling inside as I lay in my cosy single bed, though it was in the middle of a freezing cold winter. We had decided on our formal engagement and like everything else about our being together we were taking a level headed approach. We were married within the next three months. Our wedding was private, even though most of my sisters and brothers and most of Roger's living relatives were there. My sister, Althea, who comes before me in a long line of siblings dressed me and looking back now, things didn't turn out too bad considering the fact that we didn't have a great deal of time to plan and prepare for the wedding. I was only home for two weeks leave for Easter when Roger suggested we get married then instead of waiting all the way until summer as planned. It wasn't very long after we were married when Roger joined me in England and we were living in a married quarters that I realized he wasn't as sincere or caring as I thought he was.

There were two of my close friends who visited me on a regular basis, Millie from St. Vincent and Holly who is English; he constantly made it appear as if he was involved with them both. Also, he was never able to find gainful employment, in fact any measly employment he afforded himself he wasn't even able to hold onto for very long, from a few days to three months in four different jobs and that is over the five years which we were married. This reminds me of the Conflict Theory and Divorce and I quote, "Feminism stems from critical theory. It takes the perspective that socio-economic pressures ultimately create imbalance between genders. This is not a natural function of the husband/wife relationship, but a set of identities constructed for them by economic need, and which remain in conflict. Divorce can then be seen as partially or wholly a result of this perceived reality." By Jeffery St. Marie, ehow contributor, www.ehow.com/facts_7243645_conflict-theory-divorce.html.

As if things were not already bad enough, he also spent two and a half years of our marriage in the United States as he was a green card holder and was adamant that we would eventually go to live in America so he felt the need to go and make a head start but again his plans to find fruitful employment did not materialize. He continued to make it seem like he was involved with yet other female friends of mine and was never able to defend this situation very well to me when confronted so along with countless other problems which we had in our marriage, including the fact that he would not come to bed until the wee hours of the morning as he was much too happy to spend the night on the sofa in front of the television and simultaneously on the internet. I tried everything to get him to come to bed at night when I would feel lonely and confused including dressing up for him and modelling in front of the television and pleading with him but all of my efforts failed.

It was while Roger was in the United States that I met Alex, a fellow member of the Navy. I was extremely frustrated at the time in all aspects of my life and was volunteered by my Divisional Officer, Bill, to do the commemorative ceremony for Falklands in May 2007. When Bill told me about it I saw it as just another military operation that had to be done so I packed my gear and boarded my train to Portsmouth. I was based at HMS Drake in Plymouth at that time. After a few days of practice which was held on the parade grounds at HMS Excellent I was introduced by a colleague to a handsome, debonair individual who claimed he was from Jamaica but for some peculiar reason I didn't believe his claim.

Even to this day, looking back, there is still something about him that seems foreign to me. What was contradictory to my usual nature is the fact that I found him appealing mainly because of how he defended his claim. He was very forceful, his voice was very high pitched and rough and he looked like he was not at all intimidated by the fact that I was challenging him about his roots in no discrete fashion in front of hundreds of fellow Navy members of all ratings. It wasn't until much later on in that first of two weeks that I believed he was actually from Jamaica. Because it was so many of us on this operation the training accommodation was stretched to its limit so I was sharing a room which had six single beds on Britannia block with five other females. It was therefore a big favour to me when Alex told me on one occasion when we spoke, close to the end of the week that he was going home to his civilian home for the weekend and would let me have his room in one of the new blocks which housed one of the single living en-suite accommodations on the base. This was against his practise but we had spent a number of hours together talking about Jamaica, reggae music and the matter at hand, the commemorative ceremony, mainly over our meals in the cafeteria. One of his closest friends Granville was very accommodating and would allow me to take him over whenever I was alone and wanted to talk which was often since I was only there for that exercise and didn't have a lot of friends in Portsmouth.

What little friends I had in Portsmouth were away at sea. That Friday, as is pretty much the norm, we finished at noon and by the time we got back to the block everyone was busy, trying to make the most of their weekend. By 1230 I knew I had to get away from the hustle and bustle of the room and I knew the perfect place to be was in Alex's room, which had a television set, and would afford me some quiet time alone which I longed for. I was so happy with myself that I wasn't too hasty like I might have been normally and refuse the key. I remembered how I felt when he offered because I had only known him a few days, even though it felt like we had known each other for longer. Also, despite the fact that Roger was away in America for nearly two years now, I was very conscious of the fact that I was a married woman. All the time I was in his presence talking to him, I was always aware of how he would watch me keenly and constantly smiled knowingly to himself which made me feel as if he was undressing me with his eyes.

I could tell that he was a pro with women and my surety didn't come from him confiding in me that years ago when he served in an army elsewhere he had more than fifty girl friends all at the same time, but from his cool confidence. I could sense this air of surety about him; that he always got what he wanted, that everyone was satisfied with what he had to offer and that they eventually loved him and wanted more of him than he ever cared to give. This made me feel chuffed to be in his company because I knew that a man with a broad experience in the bedroom, as anyone who has watched 'Sex and the City' will agree, could make you feel the intensity of the mass of his experience with every touch of his body to yours. He was still in his block when I rang him and I awkwardly struck up a conversation though I wished I could have just asked him for the key without delay in order to make a quick get away from all the noise and confusion in my shared-room.

I eventually told him that I was accepting his offer to take the key for the weekend and I could hear the happiness in his voice as he asked me to come over to collect it. Alex's room was very cosy and smelt as fresh as a daisy. I spent the time just resting and relaxing for it had been a strenuous week. Sunday morning I woke up to the sound of birds chirping and the occasional vehicle passing below his window on the base. The atmosphere was relaxed and I became conscious I hadn't spoken to anyone for more than a day. I hungrily ate an apple, pear and banana from among the bowl of fruits he left me and a packet of Rich Tea biscuits. I started busying for something to do, with no luck I started looking around the room then I realized it. Alex's room was neat but his clothes were organized even neater. His wooden hangers in his closet were all facing in the same direction and everything was grouped in order of colour, all the whites together, all the blacks together and so on. In his drawers every piece of garment was neatly folded, even his underwear and his socks.

It struck me that I had never seen a male as neat as him before. I was moved. When he returned I had had my fare share of being alone, I was glad to have someone to talk to, someone whom I shared common interests with. He told me about his trip and I told him about my quiet weekend and we both shared jokes and exchanged laughs and before long it was time for me to return to my over crowded room, but strangely enough I didn't mind. On our last day when we went to Buckingham Palace for the Commemorative ceremony and put into practice what we had learnt over the last two weeks we spent as much time together as we could manage, sitting on the coach to and from London and waiting around for each other all the time. We were happy in each other's company and this was not only apparent to us but to others around us as well.

At the end of the assignment I went back to HMS Drake in Plymouth and Alex stayed in his respective base at HMS Nelson in Portsmouth. He spent the next four months pursuing me and I enjoyed every minute of it. We would talk and text each other constantly and it was clear we had strong feelings for each other. After the four months when Alex asked me if he could come to Plymouth and spend a weekend with me I wanted to resist like I did countless other times but my resistance was breaking down since we had grown to care for each other so much it became all the more difficult for me to put forward effective arguments to support us not spending time together but I was very much aware that us spending time together would be lethal. Roger was still away in America and I was by now living in a three bedroom house by myself.

The fact that I was talking to Alex all the time on the phone made me even more conscious of my loneliness. He always knew just the right thing to say and always made me feel so special and adored, almost like a celebrity. It was so different from the hurt and dissatisfaction I felt in my marriage. A marriage that was taking me further and further away from realising my dreams of happiness and building a life with my life-long partner. Every day after work and on the weekends I would spend my time reading, shopping or making house, always by myself and I knew deep within for a while that I wasn't going to keep this up much longer so that weekend when I finally told Alex 'Yes' and he arrived at my front door, ringing my door bell which had never been rung before and sharing the house with me which had never been shared before, while I occupied it, I knew it was destined to be something special.

But yet again, what Qupid had put his seal of approval on did not materialise. We were seeing each other for two years and we had fallen in love with each other. Unfortunately, because I was still married and Roger had returned from the USA by this time, the relationship with Alex was affecting my marriage to such an extent that I couldn't let Roger touch me anymore because it felt like I was cheating on Alex and to further complicate things I did not believe in divorce so I was forced to put an end to my affair. There was no playing down the grief and physical pain I felt when I arrived at this decision (only I hadn't told Alex about my decision) and I guess it was too much for me to pretend that the affair didn't happen. I did try to salvage my marriage but as someone very clever once said; when you have an affair you are actually making a conscious decision to end your marriage. Also, because there was a long list of other things wrong with my marriage, it was much healthier to put an end to it despite the fact that I was going against a belief I strongly held. I had a long and hard struggle with Roger to agree to and go through with the divorce. During all that I was too engulfed in my personal fight to be freed from a marriage that had gone all wrong and had neglected to keep Alex in the know and by the time the divorce had become final he resented me for shutting him out and accused me of deceiving him and not having loved him at all.

The girls were enjoying themselves and Sheldon and Beth were more than happy to be out spending time with them and taking care of them. Rosie and Melissa would go from one Ferris wheel to the next and still never seemed to get enough. They loved the colourfulness of everything around them and every chance they got in between rides they danced to the booming music. Though the surface was wet from the rain the previous day, the sun was out and the day was bright. There was always something they wanted to eat. Everything they liked was always right next to them, hot dog, ice cream, burgers, cakes, cookies and so much more.

There were food wagons with snacks all about. Children of all ages and sizes were all about and from time to time the girls would stop to glare at a child or other. Beth didn't mind supporting Melisa on her lap at times when she would be too small to sit by herself or to sit with Rosie on the ride. Sheldon looked at little Melissa as she sat on his wife's lap in the Ferris wheel they were riding on now. It was going up and down then around in circles as the girls laughed and screamed with delight. Sheldon stood out in the clearing as he looked on at them. The little girl, who had just started walking, did so briskly but she was only ten months old. She looked nothing like her mother nor anyone he had ever met. Like her sister, Rosie, she was tall for her age. Both girls had very cool complexion. Also, they had very vibrant and polite personalities.

I was jerked back to the present by my phone which was ringing louder than ever now. I knew that I could not afford to avoid George's call because even though we had text each other several times throughout the day, he would take it the wrong way and I couldn't afford for that to happen. I had skylarked long enough with the men in my life whom I loved and I wasn't about to let it happen again. I grabbed up the phone just seconds before it stopped ringing and tried to say hello but only my lips moved, there were no words coming out of my mouth and I knew I was not going to be able to say much if anything at all. He knew I was there at the other end because he could tell that the line was open.

"Hello," he said, and waited but no answer came. There was a cold chill in my stomach and I hoped he wouldn't hang up, but how would he know. "Hello, are you there Marge?" He asked in a most understanding and sincere voice and that's when I found the courage. "Yes, I'm here," I said in a frail and insecure voice that made me feel so stupid. I didn't know what to expect now. I thought that maybe he would be disappointed and hang up and I would never hear from him again. "Marge, why didn't you answer me?" he asked in a quiet tone. "I thought you didn't want to talk to me," he said. "No, that's not it," I tried to explain and I could feel tears welling up inside my eyes because the last thing I wanted to do was to hurt him.

"Is it a bad time for you, would you like me to ring you back at another time," he asked sincerely and I hastily shouted, "No! Don't go, I'm free to talk. I was just a bit nervous that's all." "Then why didn't you say so?" He asked in a matter-of-fact tone of voice and then he went on to soothe and calm me down just as I imagined he would do. He had a strong but kind voice, a remarkable accent, a way with words and a warm and loving personality. By talking to him I felt like the sun was shining its warm beautiful ray down on me though it was winter and the evenings were turning into nights earlier and earlier. I was relaxed now and started to enjoy our conversation as I answered George's question.

"What are you looking for in a husband?" he asked seriously. I paused to think for a second and then answered, "A loving, faithful, caring, honest and sincere man who is good with children and is madly in love with me." "That sounds pretty much like what I'm looking for in a wife." He said. We went on talking for over an hour which seemed to go so fast and by the time he said, "I like you Marge, I really hope we are able to meet each other soon." I felt like I had only just started talking, except for the fact that I was nervous again from the prospect of meeting him face to face.

OUR FIRST MEETING

It was one week since George and I had our first conversation over the phone and since that first evening we made it a habit to talk on the phone every night. We were so comfortable with each other and also we had become dependent on each other for company. We were talking a lot on the phone but we still hadn't lost the old appeal for texting each other so we were still doing a lot of that as well. I was not only getting to know George better but I was also learning about his family that he holds dear to him. His father who died a painful death from cancer, his mom whom he loves sincerely who suffers from diabetes, his older sister Robin, his adorable and very courageous little sister, Susan and his little brother who died from the heart break of losing his father. He confided in me how much he loved children and was longing for the day when he would have some of his own. I told him that I was from a large family of twelve children and he marvelled at the size of my family. I explained that he would have to be prepared for large crowds whenever we had family gatherings if he was to contend with me and he laughed joyously.

I told him one or two stories of my upbringing, growing up with eleven siblings and how my parents had many struggles bringing us up, not in the countryside where it would have been easier to support us, as we would have grown our own provisions, but instead in Payton Place, a tiny area, just above August Town which is opposite to the University of the West Indies (UWI), Mona Campus. August Town is a residential community, an eastern suburb of Kingston, Jamaica. My mother's family originally have their roots in August Town where her parents (my grandparents) met, fell in love, married and produced five children, four girls and one boy, the youngest of which is my mother. August Town is a massive region and is made up of several smaller communities each differentiated by its distinct culture.

My grandfather was a soldier in the Jamaica Defence Force (JDF) and was known and respected by everyone in the community for his bravery and industriousness. He paid his dues in the world war and when he eventually died was buried by the JDF. The funeral service was held in the community and everyone attended from far and wide to show their last respects. The streets were full with mourners and the burial ground, just a stone throw from what was his home, was way too small for the event.

My mother left the community when she met my father who was from rural St. Elizabeth, Jamaica. My father worked at the UWI Students' Union for his entire life and was the most committed, hard working and punctual individual I have ever known. He never took a day off work, not for any reason, and he was never late, not even once. I remember when I was growing up my father would listen for the alarm (a loud howling sound lasting for about one minute), which the UWI used on the campus to signal the beginning of each work-day. Though this alarm is used mainly by the thousands of students and staff on the campus, it is used widely by the people in the community as well. The UWI is staffed mainly by people from the August Town community who are both white and blue collar, even academic staff.

In fact two of my most brilliant lecturers while I attended the University were born and bred in August Town and proudly so. A vast proportion of the students who commute to the Campus and even some of those who live in the various halls are from August Town. Two of my cousins Jacob and Kim who were born and bred in the August Town community attended the UWI at the same time that I attended the university and have attained outstanding degrees. In fact Jacob, who also is a product of the August Town Primary school, was at one time the president of the Student Union. The alarm would go off at 0730 and as soon as it would sound my father would drop whatever he was doing and quickly make his exit even though his walk to work took ten minutes and he wasn't expected at work until 0800. It is said that this alarm, which the neighbourhood people call "Quashi", was installed during the period of slavery and that the large, scenic grounds of the campus was a cane field where slaves worked long and hard, shedding blood, sweat and tears.

While serving in the Navy, I remember the first time the siren went off for Actions Stations. I was going about my usual routine and heard this loud howling familiar sound and immediately remembered 'Quashi' back in Jamaica, oddly enough, it was a pretty similar sound. August Town is popular for Bedwardism. The main catalyst, which is responsible for transforming the revivalist sects into a mass movement, Alexander Bedward, was born and bred in August Town. The August Town Primary school is located in the heart of the community. The community also has its own football club which is performing outstandingly and currently plays in the National Premier League. Reggae artists such as Sizzla Kalonji and new comer Duane Stephenson are also products of the community.

From my detailed description of my born land, my beautiful, beautiful Jamaica, which is the largest English speaking Caribbean Island, is a small but powerful island which has its history in the creation and advancement of the reggae music, a rich and flourishing tourist industry and a gifted and talented people. A true legend of the music is Bob Marley and many others of a similar calibre. In athletics there is a countless number of stalwarts, two of these are Merlene Ottey and Donald Quarrie. Also, be-known worldwide for their athletics ability, are certain stamina daddies, such as Usain Bolt and Asafa Powell.

My little brother Sheldon Style is also a truly gifted athlete, who himself has represented Jamaica worldwide, even earned himself a scholarship and has studied and done very well at the USA's distinguished Morehouse College. Upon hearing about Jamaica, as I babbled on, glad finally for the chance to talk about a truly amazing place, George purred comfortably at the other end of the phone and said. "I sure would love to visit Jamaica one day and I also would love to meet your family." I was chuffed. I thought to myself, "I haven't even begun to tell him all about Jamaica and my upbringing yet." I decided to give it a rest for the meantime. "Marge," he said hesitantly, and I waited quietly for him to finish. "Is it alright?" He started, "I would love to meet you in person, are you doing anything this weekend, how about Saturday evening at 1900?"

I was speechless but I was used to talking with George all the time now so it was not as bad as before. I took a minute to assert myself and replied confidently, "I would love to meet you in person too, where are we going?" "Do you like Indian food?" He asked. "I love Indian food." I said and I could hear him smile through the phone. That evening as I prepared for bed I was so happy, happier than I had been in a long time but I was apprehensive too. I knew that he could see me and then decide that he wasn't interested in me and that would really hurt because I also knew that I liked him a lot and already had a vision of him in my future.

On Saturday at 1825 I looked out the lounge window anxiously but there was no one there. A moment later I got up from the sofa and began to pace the floor eagerly but in no time at all the doorbell sounded resoundingly and made me jump with fright. The taxi travelled along the M6 in the direction of the restaurant and I sat nervously looking at my watch every minute in the back seat of the large black car. I knew that I would get there in good time and be safely seated before I would have to worry about meeting George. I thought about the day's events and was glad now that instead of conversing with George for an extended length of time I had saved most of my time for preparing myself, "But did I look good enough for George to be happy with me?" I wondered. I definitely pulled out all the stops for this one.

I got up at 0600 as usual, had my breakfast and though I didn't do job search on the weekend I still felt the need to utilize my time very carefully, so I avoided the television and went straight to my closet. It was a sliding, double glass door closet which was placed strategically, directly in front of my bed so I could see myself at all times from my bed. Clothes were hung on the rails on both sides and there were shelves at the top above the hanging clothes where I keep my head gears, for example, my Royal Navy cap with my HMS York cap tally still on it, among other accessories, as well as at the bottom below the hanging clothes where I keep my footwear. I reached up and took down three boxes carefully placed to the very back of the closet, from within them I got out my little hot numbers, my varsace, prada and dolce and gabbana, all glamorous, couture dresses, with shoes and hand bags to match.

I thanked the Lord now that while I was in the Navy I had put away a little something for a rainy day; my brand named gears. Even though I didn't have a lot of them and had them now over a year I knew that money well spent, regardless of how long ago, on quality clothes would never be regretted. With the rising prices I never would be able to buy them today. There were three sets, a black, a red and a white one. Dresses that cling adequately to my body without showing off too much, they were cut just above the knees and they all looked elegant; elegant enough to give me a touch of class when I dolled up, which I have reserved for only very special occasions. I hadn't worn them yet so I was particularly careful, taking my time to avoid damaging them in any way. I knew that I had to choose one to wear tonight and I was more than prepared to try them all on to see which one fits best. I also had to hurry to get to my hair dresser's appointment for 1000 which I usually do on a Saturday to get my hair specially shampooed and my French manicured nails done. I wanted to be able to relax for a bit in the warm aromatherapy bath foam while I do my oatmeal facial, before I'd have to start rushing around to put on perfectly made-up make up and sliding into my dress.

I couldn't afford to be late and at the same time I needed as much time as I could be afforded as I just had to look and be at my very best this evening. I looked down at my dress in the taxi now and I was glad with my choice, I had chosen the black dress, mainly because, though I had been in the Navy and was pretty fit during my tenure, my stomach was not as flat as it used to be so I pulled on a gut buster knickers I collected from Marks & Spencer, which didn't leave a bulge in my dress at all, one reason was because I was wearing black and the other was that though the knickers gave support to my waist and made it look firm and tight it was also a thong so the part which hugged my well proportioned, rounded buttocks was fashionable and looked modest by the time it left a very discrete pattern through my black dress.

Everything had gone to plan. My thick black hair looked jet black and shiny by the time it was straightened and my nails looked clean and hygienic. I was out of the bath within an hour and I could feel the benefit as I was completely rejuvenated and now feeling calm and collective. I had used my share cover make up which I ordered and had delivered in the post a few months earlier and finished by spraying a hint of Chanel Mademoiselle perfume behind my ears. I definitely felt I was looking hot when I stood in front of the long closet mirrors in my bedroom, which boosted my confidence a bit but anything could still go wrong because my appearance, though I had put so much effort into it might not be of George's liking.

I looked at my watch and it was 1850 and I knew the restaurant was close now and instantaneously I could feel a chill in my stomach. A moment later the taxi dragged to a halt in front of a magnificent restaurant with high glass structure. The word "Nawaab" was written in large letters made bright by fluorescent light. I could see straight through the glass into the spacious, well decorated, cosy lounge. A number of affluent and well groomed people moved about inside, some sitting about on the cushioned sofas, while others stood, watching the door, eagerly awaiting their company. Still, others were entering and a few satisfied looking people were leaving the restaurant. I regrouped and collected myself, grabbed my purse, paid the driver, who was a middle-aged man with a kind face and went into the spinning doors.

I moved as swiftly as I could among the people who were coming and going, making sure to hold my head down so no one could see my face. I just wanted to be seated at a table and then I would feel comfortable enough to call George on his mobile and tell him where I was. During our last conversation he wanted to know what I was wearing and for fear that he might recognize me I told him that I preferred to surprise him. I was almost at the end of the lounge and felt relieved that I had made it but as I stretched out my hand to push open the second door leading to the dining area I heard a strong and secure voice say, "Marge, wait, I'm over here!" I was gobsmacked.

I couldn't believe he recognized me and was so sure of himself as well because even though I had sent him a number of pictures I just didn't think they were clear enough for him to recognize me in person. My throat locked and my knees along with it and I felt as vulnerable as a newborn baby as I glanced up and saw a tall, muscular figure quickly approaching and felt his hand grip mine. His voice sounded just as melodious and caring as it did on the phone and his hand which gently took mine into its powerful grip and expertly led me away from the door and to the sofa where I was seated so fast my body had no time to react.

"Marge," he was saying, "I am so happy to finally meet you. I wanted to meet you from the first time I spoke to you on the phone but I didn't want to ask you too early and risk scaring you away, you see." He was looking so genuine and sincere as I looked deep into his big, bright, brown eyes. He was very handsome and so charming as he stared at me with piercing eyes, willing me to say something. I wanted to say so much and my mouth opened, only to close again as the words just wouldn't come. He must have realized something was wrong because he embraced me, closing his big, powerful body around me and as he blocked out all the eyes which were glaring at us I felt safe.

"It's alright, you can talk to me Marge, I will never hurt you." He said in my ear and my body became miraculously relaxed as if he had willed it so. I began to think to myself of the last time someone was ever so kind, gentle and caring towards me and I couldn't remember. Tears welled up in my eyes as I remembered my divorce and how painful it was, my entire personal life was like a river of pain and I could still feel the hurt like it was yesterday. I knew I had to pull myself together; this was not the time to break-down. "I have to show him that I am a strong, ex-military woman, just like he likes me to be," I thought. I pulled myself away, which took all of my strength; in fact I was surprised I had it in me because he was as strong as a horse, resting solid against my bosom.

I noticed, as he sat next to me, for the first time that he was wearing a navy blue close fitted body top, showing off his six packs and a pair of black jeans which anyone would believe to be regular trousers unless they looked really closely at it. On his feet he wore a very neat black pair of sneakers which looked a lot like shoes. I wanted to run back into his embrace and set up permanent residence there, where I would never ever let him go but I knew too well that if I wanted to keep him I would have to be strong, brave and confident, just as the Navy would have me be. I squared my shoulders and threw my head back as I reached for my confidence deep in my stomach and in a cool, jovial voice I said, "I am happy to meet you too George and I've enjoyed out telephone conversations, please forgive me, I was just a bit surprised, that's all." He reached for my hand again as he watched my face, my hand was putty in his, and he said in an assuring voice. "You don't have to apologise to me Marge, alright, don't worry, I understand." I knew then and there that I was in safe hands and I happily let him take the lead. "I reserved our table a few days ago hoping that you would say yes, so we can go in whenever you are ready."My heart leapt as I replied, "We should go then, I am famished!"

He kept my hand safely in his as we stood up without further delay, in unison and purposefully walked through the inner door, where, below on the large landing at least a hundred tables were well laid out and all but a few were not occupied. Within minutes we were seated at a cosy side table for two. We talked quietly and joyously to each other as we had our delicious meal and barely took notice of it as our eyes were planted on each other and we might as well have had our date in the middle of nowhere, as long as the two of us were together it was enough. He complimented me on my beauty and it puzzled me for I had never been praised before in quite the same way. As he said, with his wonderful, delightful, English accent, "Marge, you are beautiful." A part of me died and came back to being more vibrant than before.

I longed to get lost in his arms but I knew I had to be patient and take things slowly. "Thank you, you are very handsome." But he had moved beyond my compliment and was now telling me he thinks he has finally found himself the perfect wife after his many years of searching and that he now feels he can finally settle down and have the family he has always wanted. George embraced me again as we said goodbye and prepared to leave. As I walked to the lounge I marvelled at how very happy and secure I felt.

Tom, the taxi driver returned for me and was waiting for me when I got to the lounge and I was relieved because I was now too tired to resist any more offers from George to take me home. I knew I had to be careful not to be alone with him because I couldn't depend on myself to be strong and I wasn't sure if he himself was strong in this regard. As I travelled back in the taxi I thought of how much I enjoyed myself. I remember prior to my date how I fussed and worried about my appearance and whether George would approve of it but now I realize how foolish I had been. I was pleased with myself for the first time in a long time and that night I slept soundly and blissfully.

The girls were collected on a quiet, sunny day from their uncle and aunt's in Old Harbour where they thoroughly enjoyed their stay; they were not too happy to leave as they were constantly petted and pampered but again were defeated by their sense of adventure. They were collected by their aunt Althea who whisked them away to Greater Portmore in no time at all. As soon as they arrived at the house which was located within a small secured community they scampered out of the car and into the house where they found their cousins Cal and Collin and had a loud, joyous reunion. The boys were very happy to see them and immediately invited them to play on their wii console.

It was electrifying as they discussed everything from the game they were playing, to the girls' flight, to their visits with their other aunts and uncles. Melissa, whom the entire Style family was only meeting for the first time was a bit young for it all but she just babbled along and laughed when everyone else was laughing and soon she became the centre of attention with everyone hugging her and trying to lift her up. Rosie on the other hand was very mature for her age and so she had no problems conversing with twenty-one years old Collin and of course nine years old Cal who was so grown up since the last time she saw him. She thought back to the days when she went to Vaz Prep school with Cal like he was her own brother and she missed having company to go to school with, in fact she missed him a lot but she refused to mention it. She was now just doing her best to beat the boys at their wii game and she was just about to when they were all called into the dining room for their evening meal.

Althea who was trained as a beautician laid out a delicious treat of ackee and salt fish and dumplings and green bananas for them on the table and a large array of cakes, puddings and pies for dessert and they knew right off that in order to get their very enticing dessert they would have to first finish their main course so they quickly dived in each competing with the other in an effort to get to the dessert first. Althea ran her own beauty salon for years but gave it up recently in order to partner with her husband, Jeff. Jeff, who graduated from university several years earlier and started his own wholesale food business was more than happy to have his wife on board with him where they could work together and spend time in each others company all day.

NAVY DAYS

One fine day, on yet another of my priceless, most enjoyable dates with George, this time he invited me for a Sunday picnic followed by a movie later in the evening. I thought about how remote the park would be but I didn't feel intimidated by this because I had gone on numerous dates prior to this one with George and was now extremely comfortable and happy with him. I was certain now, without a doubt that I was in love with him and that he was feeling the same way. It was a pleasant Sunday afternoon. It was very quiet and sunny and we laid out our small containers of home cooked food on George's large multi-coloured plaid blanket which he had earlier spread on the grass in the middle of the large country park.

The surface all around us was dry though the vegetation was mostly green and healthy looking. I observed the blue bells and lilies and even the big bright sun flowers as we sat close enough to each other for me to sniff the glorious fresh scent of George's Lynx shower jell and wish I could embrace him without seeming needy. I looked into his handsome face and wondered what he was thinking as he stared back at me quizzically. "Marge, penny for your thoughts," he said quietly as he reached for a second slice of my specially made cheese cake.

Though, while serving in the Navy, I loved the role of the military in defending its country in various different realms and had no qualms in performing my duties and responsibilities in fulfilling this role, the memories most imprinted on my mind now that I have moved on from that chapter of my life are my early experiences during my very first few months in the Navy, while I endured the countless challenges of naval training and later, that of docking in various wharfs overseas, while experiencing the cultures and scenic beauty of these formerly strange lands.

It was on the morning of the 30th June 2003 that I nervously departed the seemingly controversial neighbourhood of Openshaw in Manchester with my small suitcase. The bus ride seemed unusually short this morning and so did the train ride as the Virgin train made its way from across Lancashire in the north to Plymouth in the south of England. The day had surprisingly brightened up from being blistering cold and rainy in the wee hours of the morning as I boarded the train from Manchester Piccadilly station. I must have been tired from the journey because I awoke to the sound of the train driver's crystal clear voice informing us that we were arriving at Plymouth station. I jumped out of sleep, collected my head from the glass window and looked around quickly to see if it was time for me to get off the train.

The sun was shining brightly and as I stood out on the platform and felt the cool fresh air caressing my face I knew that this would definitely be the start of something vitally special. After all, I was starting my Naval training, it was the beginning of my Naval career. I went into this cute little cafe and waited by the sign which was written on a blackboard that read, "Wait here to be collected by the Navy". It wasn't long before I was collected along with a handful of other individuals and seated in a large coach which was full of other new recruits. The bus drove hastily past the town centre and all the way to the ferry which we took to the other side, where we were collected by a second bus which took us just as hastily to HMS Raleigh.

It was at this point I briefly relived the last few months of my life. I thought about my last few months at university, my personal training that I did in order to get myself ready for the Navy's training and last but by no means least, my family and their reaction to my plan to join the Royal Navy. The lectures at university always made you pregnant with knowledge and filled you with high expectations and hope for the future. Ever since I can remember I was always a good student and it was no different while I was at university, I would stay up until late at night studying and preparing for my intense and informative lectures and tutorials of the next day. It was even worse in my last semester because I knew I had no time to re-do any of my courses if I were to fail any of them as I only had a few weeks after the end of the semester to prepare myself and take my long flight to England.

I was really into physical fitness as well, ever since I was accepted to join the Navy in the summer of 2002. After ending my relationship with Chris and returning to Jamaica to complete my degree I made sure I went and got a total gym exercising machine from Courts and I used it twice daily. I also ran more than four miles each day at the University bowl and swam at least twice weekly in the University's pool. I was mega fit by the time I arrived in England and sat on that bus to Raleigh.

I remember how worried my family was when I told them I was going to join the Royal Navy. They knew I was due to finish my degree at the end of that academic year and were looking for me to take up fruitful employment in Jamaica where I could save and invest in a mortgage and a nice car in good time, which is typical of what university graduates do in Jamaica. But instead I opted to migrate and join the Royal Navy which they thought was a risky way of life for me and since I was educated in Jamaica, that this kind of attitude was causing brain drain to the Jamaican economy.

On the Monday afternoon when I finally packed the last of my stuff, among them was the list of things I was asked to take for my Naval training I knew that I would never return to live in Jamaica. It was a bright, sunny day and all the members of my family came back to the main house, where we were all born, at Payton Place to bid me farewell begrudgingly. I said farewell to my beloved country, the country of my birth which nourished and cherished me all my years. I felt a bit sad at the idea but I knew that I had waited for this day to come for a long time; my entire last year at university, changing my mind at this point was just out of the question.

My friend Kelly, whom I met at University and knew for some years now was taking me to Kingston's Norman Manley airport. She glanced over at me and read my face straight away. "You know what?" she said, "I'll be coming to England too." "Really?" I asked, I was gobsmacked. She explained that she had been looking into the idea ever since I told her I was joining the Royal Navy and had decided a few weeks earlier so now she would be arriving in a few months. I was so happy and relieved because now I was going to have a friend with me in England, someone who I could call upon to share in both my good and bad times.

The traffic that evening was at a stand still for most of the journey as we went on about the things we would do and the time we would spend together, without realizing how much time had passed. By the time I got to the check in counter I was informed that I had missed my flight. This was very bad news because every penny that I had was tightly budgeted and I didn't want to have to bother my family for money to upgrade my ticket.

I remember like it was yesterday, the well groomed, petite flight attendant as she came forward as soon as I reached the front of the queue to inform me that it would cost me US$100 to upgrade my ticket. My mouth went dry and I knew straight away that I would have to get the money from somewhere other than my own cash.

I decided to call Roger, against my better judgement as we were quite close at the time but I didn't want to burden him. Something that I will never be able to forget as long as I live is how quickly Roger came to my aid. I remember asking him shyly on his mobile and right away he said, "Yes, where are you?" I told him and even though he was miles away when we spoke he was by my side in no time and upgrading my ticket for me. I was flabbergasted.

As I travelled to Raleigh there was only one thing that distracted me from memories of my recent past, my friend Tiffany whom I met on the same day I travelled to Raleigh for the first time, I felt delighted to be in her company because we seemed to have a lot in common as we talked to each other for the first time. We were always there for each other throughout our arduous training among others such as Cody, whom I knew from the previous summer, actually, she is the one who told me about the Navy and encouraged me to join up when I was in England in 2002 on holiday. Lucy, who Tiffany and I met at some point during part one training and decided to make our friend and there were others who were our friends but who were not as close to us during training like Tessa, Megan, Meisha, Pete and a host of others.

I remember Tiffany on that first day like it was yesterday. As we piled off the bus and onto the ferry, I spotted her and thought to myself that she looked like a typical Jamaican, in her mini jeans skirt and her almost mid-drift like brown blouse, she was tall and slim. I gave her a faint smile and she didn't even budge but just stood there looking a bit annoyed and I felt a bit uncomfortable talking to someone with this kind of mannerism but I just have this very curious nature where I just have to find out. I later realized that she means absolutely nothing by the mannerism she portrayed to me that day, but that that was just her disposition. Looking back now, I bet she is probably not even aware of it.

The first order of the day when we arrived at HMS Raleigh was new entry which lasted for one week where you familiarize yourself with people of similar rate as yourself, learn the basic rules of survival within a military institution and essentially, practicing good time keeping. When Cody and I met in summer 2002, we became good friends fast, we met purely by accident as I got lost one day while staying with Chris in his dorm. Chris was gone to his daily morning classes and I made a quick run to the shopping centre, which wasn't very far away, but on my way back I got a bit lost.

I saw this fashionable, petite young lady going past me, I stopped her and tried to get directions from her, she was very helpful and then she asked at the end "where are you from?" "I'm from Jamaica." I said, as she retorted, "I'm from Trinidad." We hit it off right away and exchanged mobile numbers. It was shortly after that, that she told me about the Navy and of her plans to join up. I was more than happy to join up myself because I always wanted to join the military. Also, I wanted desperately to get away from everything that was familiar to me because it was shortly after Cody and I met that I broke up with Chris and as a result, everything in my life seemed diabolical.

Part one training mainly focussed on physical fitness which was very challenging and exciting in every way. Every aspect of it was strenuous and demanded all your will power and stamina. It gave you such a powerful feeling of victory inside just to be able to survive each day and get through to the next day. It was the daily gym work out, the grinding marching on the parade ground regardless of the weather, finger peeling and mind boggling hand washing, ironing and A4 folding of all your kit, the constant and long suffering buffing of all your shoes and boots for endless number of kit inspections, the lengthy lessons which you were meant to revise each night for your weekly tests and the countless miles of body numbing walk to pier cellars and Dartmouth with all your kit stashed to your back. All these activities and still others not mentioned are carried out in order to strengthen and discipline both the body and mind of the recruit. I remember one evening after meal everyone was anxious to get their kit into tick-tack condition for the next morning and as always, first were the foot wears which had to be buffed for hours until they were crispy clean and perfectly shiny.

Everyone grabbed their foot wears, cotton balls and black polish and sat down in two neat lines along the long corridor facing each other as they worked hurriedly and competitively, always conscious of the fact that they had numerous chores yet to do before dropping into bed in a pile just in time for lights out at 2200 sharp nightly and rounds which follow to check everyone is in her bed. There was this kind of mature, slightly chubby girl amongst us who would remind you of just an ordinary girl next door, words had it that she had crossed over from the Royal Air force

(RAF) and had just split up with her partner of several years as well, she was called Mandy and at that time what we did not know was that soon she would become the class leader of Pellow Division. For a split second there was silence from the usual muttering and complaints among the girls about the day's affairs and everyone heard as Mandy said in a really puzzled voice, to no one in particular, "What am I doing here?" I was shocked when almost all, if not everyone agreed with her because that is exactly how I felt from the very first day I entered the gates of HMS Raleigh, I was always surprised that nothing in my life prior to this had prepared me for life in the Navy in the least. Don't get me wrong. I wanted nothing more than to join the Navy for all the right reasons, you see.

From I was a young girl growing up, watching all those black and white war movies I always felt I had to serve in the military to fulfil a strong desire within me to be courageous, disciplined and patriotic in defending my country. Later on when I tried to pursue this dream, after finishing high school, my family's strong Christian values and beliefs got in the way and so I was strongly discouraged. As a result, it was several years afterwards that my dream was accomplished. Of course, the income, benefits, comradeship and the fact that the Navy is so prestigious may not all normally be positive motivators but in the case of the Royal Navy they are. After enough time passed though, we became institutionalized, in terms of what we ate, wore, our language and attitude. Everything had taken on a military theme, then you realize what being in the Navy is all about and by this time you don't ask anymore if the team works, you know it has to work because this means so much to you. I learnt fast that the quality of the friendships and relationships you build during your time in training is what determine the quality of your stay throughout your years in the service.

Also, your performance during training is fundamentally the backdrop to your performance that follows in the service. I was very good at track and field during part one training and always was the first female to finish in our regular track and field tests, this carried through to the rest of my time in the Navy and I always did excellently in my fitness tests. Swimming was my weak area throughout part one training and I failed my swimming test once but took it again thirty minutes later and passed it.

My motivation was I realized that all my friends and colleagues with Caribbean heritage had failed and I just couldn't sit with this so I asked for a second test and came close to drowning but decided that I wasn't leaving the water until I passed. The test wasn't like any ordinary swimming test.

You had to swim the full length of the pool then half way back thread water for three minutes in your heavy overalls and high leg combat boots with socks and all. As if that wasn't bad enough, what made it even more difficult to pass the test was the fact that the water was hard water which felt toxic when you are doing your swimming test and we were used to soft water in the Caribbean.

My Divisional Officer, who watched from the seats above, later told me he had never seen anyone as determined as me before. I was not very popular among the girls in my division, Cunningham Division, because they thought I was showing up their shortcomings and making things complicated for them. There is this song "complicated" by Avril Lavigne, which they would play on my behalf whenever we were in the dorm for any length of time. They would always play prank on me like hiding the day's programme so I wouldn't know what was taking place and so I wouldn't be able to make crucial preparations.

As a result I learnt from very early in my naval tenure to always prepare myself for any eventualities which called for more work but always paid off in the end. I remember times when we were all at our wits end and we would play the "Kentucky fried chicken and a pizza hut song" and sing along with it at the top of our lungs. When we had our passing in ceremony from part one into part two training I felt like a fish out of water because I was the only one who had no family or friends attending to support me in passing such a major milestone in my Naval training.

Everyone had their immediate family there to show off, introduce around and take pictures with. The people who had the most fun were those who had a military family background, these people had everyone looking on in awe and admiration as their dad and brother(s) and in extreme cases mom and sister(s) as well were dressed in military uniforms adorned by official gold stripes, cap tally's and badges. Others are those with their families well dressed in couture attire and expensive suits which implied that they were well represented. The passing in ceremony was definitely an affair, everyone's family who attended just seemed to make such an effort to look their best and be on their best behaviour for the day. Though I personally felt a bit out of place that day as my family was unable to attend to see me pass into part two training, I couldn't help admiring the togetherness and supportiveness between the trainees and their families.

I was rescued yet again by Charlton on that faithful day. He is someone I always admired who seems to always help me out in times of crises, a trainee in the same division as myself who is always very humble and is a great young man. Everyone was surprised at the passing in ceremony when they realized that his father was a high ranking officer in the Navy and he was more or less from an affluent background though he never disclosed this to anyone. He invited me over to have my meal with his dad, mom, young brother and two sisters. I was well received by them as he introduced me to them in a very sincere fashion, his father stood up and shook my hand; his mom smiled warmly and put me at ease and his young siblings said hello politely. They involved me in all their conversations. The sub-total of what he did for me back then can only be described as priceless.

Part two training mainly had to do with focussing on your main area of work you'll be involved in after training and therefore was academic based. I was awarded the position of Class Leader in part two training which came as no surprise because, as I said earlier, I am a good student, so it wasn't difficult coming first in almost all the written tests given. Surprisingly, I did not enjoy this part of training as much as I enjoyed part one training which involved mostly physical activities while part two training only involved very minimal amount of physical activities. The first part of part two training I enjoyed, not because of the training itself, no, but because of a guy called Micky.

During my first week in Ceres Division, which is where the Logistician Supply Chain (Stores Accountants/SA), Logistician Personnel (Writers), Catering (Chefs and Stewards) go to pursue their professional training, we were doing a bit of physical activities and by chance I spotted him. He was handsome and has a very nice personality but he was not my usual kind of guy. I think the attraction came because I was looking for something to detract me from my reality at the time. It may have been the same for him, I don't know, but we both seemed to catch each others eyes at the same time. Micky was not very tall but of slim built, dark and handsome. He was clever and had piercing eyes. That cold September day when I first saw him during a track and field exercise of about one hundred and fifty recruits of Ceres Division, it was his bow legs and piercing eyes which caught my attention. Funny how half the time if you want to catch a guy's attention all you have to do is to stare at him.

After that track and field exercise I noticed he was searching for me every evening when we returned from our daily training. It took a while to realize it but wherever I was, whether I was at the Raleigh bar hanging out with friends, the Spar shop buying supplies I'd need to sort out my kit, at the SA school studying or just wandering about aimlessly on the base he would always find me and would just stare at me with his piercing eyes. Round about October time he would start saying hello and making an attempt at small talk and by this time I was feeling like all my chances of a social life had been shot so I was happy to be getting the attention. I was spending more and more time at the SA school studying until late for my weekly exams and since the school was a bit of a distance away from our mess (large room within which several male or female recruits live) we agreed that he would collect me from the school and we would walk back to the mess together. Sometimes he would get there early and just sit and wait until I was finished studying or at other times he would help me to study.

At night when we would walk back together we would share any issues of concern we had with each other which we felt helped us as it broadened our social support systems. Pretty soon we started talking about our personal lives and I told him about Roger who was a very good friend of mine for many years who called me every day since I arrived in England and he in return told me about his expectant wife whom he loved and missed so much and how he longed to be with her and wanted to be there for the birth of their baby. At times he would be upset with his wife who would make demands that he couldn't fulfil at that point in time and this would leave him feeling inadequate and troubled. It was one of these evenings that he spoke to me about having an argument with her and I could see he was weighed down with it all so when we got up close to each other and connected in embrace, it just felt like we were supporting each other, then without any anticipation of what was coming, our lips found each other and before we knew it we were standing out in the cold, under the moon light, entangled in each others embrace and passionately kissing.

Were it not for a Petty Officer making his hourly rounds of the premises, God bless his soul, so sexually frustrate we were that I think we would have gone much further that night. Shortly after that night Micky had successfully completed his professional training and got posted to London. So good he was that he came back to Raleigh one weekend to visit all his friends who were still there. Majority of trainees that pass out never keep their promises to return for visits. It was not long afterwards that I got posted to HMS Seahawk at RNAS Culdrose.

I cried the day when I was told I was being drafted to RNAS Culdrose but the good thing about Cornwall is that even though it rains an awful lot the golden-sun shines almost every day and there is always a beautiful beach nearby. The atmosphere is peaceful and quite and the country wind is always twirling about your face and blowing your clothes to and fro. Cornwall is beautiful but sometimes the quietness is hard to bear.

After a very eventful two years at the Naval Stores office at RNAS Culdrose, my travels to various parts of the world began, thanks to the Royal Navy, which, as I said during my first introductory speech while I was in Naval training and still believe today "The Royal Navy is a most prestigious institution". I was drafted to a unit called RFANSU at RNAS Culdrose where I worked on RFA Fort George and Fort Victoria. While on either one of those ships I got the precious opportunity to visit France, Gibraltar and Norway. While I was back working on the base my only reprieve was to go on regular nights out with a few friends who knew how to dance and make themselves the stars of the party. That would be Samantha, Jim, Max and Ken. We had many brilliant nights out together in Plymouth's Candy store and Revolutions among other night clubs.

I remember Brest, the most western part of Brittany, in France like it was yesterday. Brest has its location in a natural harbour and has loads of ancient architecture. I remember going from one small clothing and souvenir shop to another, with their colourful display of items. The sun was out for most of the day as large crowds of people attracted by bargain prices continually strolled through the market which was mainly along the streets. My colleagues and I strolled along with the crowds through the streets and into several souvenir shops as we tried to find suitable gifts to take back for our families and friends but we didn't find exactly what we wanted until, though time consuming, we shopped around in the market. I bought a small beautifully painted trinket box for my special little one and a set of brightly coloured handkerchief for Roger. I was always careful not to spend too much. The sun disappeared from sight and the air blew cool as we strolled back to the dock as evening drew close. By night fall everyone was in their best attire and sat in the nearest Irish pub, which I came to accept as a Naval tradition, as long as there was an Irish pub on whichever land we visited we had to spend the greater part of the night in it before going pub hopping.

My next stop was Gibraltar which is a British overseas territory and was once a base for the Navy. It is connected to the north with Spain and has a population of 30,000. I was in the ship's aft navigational office observing and recording the aircrafts arrivals and departures for an all day training exercise for pilots. I was a bit nervous because from were I sat I could see the aircrafts coming straight at me. It was a bit surreal as numerous flights of sea kings search and rescue aircrafts, hercules, black hawks, merlins, lynx and others kept coming in. It was dangerously exciting. Most of them would turn on either of their sides and do somersaults or turn upside down as they neared the ship then they would land briefly before taking off again for their next round or some would just hover long enough to get sorted and take off again.

So busy I was, caught up with the exercise and had just put my head in the notebook long enough to record some details that I didn't see when Gibraltar crept upon us from out of nowhere. There it was, it just appeared and was all around the ship like a beautifully painstakingly hand created artwork; it was like a fairy tale. The entire island was all around the ship, it all seemed so close. I was gobsmacked. Later on, in the evening I went out to have a look and first went to the cemetery which was used throughout the 1914-1918 War for the burial of sailors and soldiers who died on ships passing Gibraltar, or those who died in the Military Hospital. It was very touching to see the names of those heroes who fought and gave their lives, neatly scrawled on their very clean and well kept head stones, all in rows both vertically and horizontally. I then went to the rocks and looked down for a while at the steep terrain, and later walked along the beautiful beach.

Finally, while on that draft I went to Norway, a scandinavian country full of beautiful fjords with tall mountains and glaciers. Norway is the second largest exporter of seafood. It was first thing in the morning when we docked up in Christiansand. It was obvious that it had snowed heavily the night before as the snow was at least three feet high and the air was freezing. Our fingers were numb and our faces turned red or purple as we worked hurriedly outside the ship in the dockyard. By the time we changed for the evening our visit to the nearest pub was long over due. The people we met that night were very pleasant and made us feel right at home even when they didn't speak much English. I recall bubbling away to one of Sean Paul's songs "Gimme the light", at one point after a beer or two, with a bunch of my colleagues from off the ship cheering me on, it doesn't take much to make me tipsy. I found that wherever we went there was always at least the odd one reggae song played which was enough to make me happy. The music though mostly foreign was good and as it were, it was a good night out. We walked back later in the snow quietly discussing the night's events.

At the time both my shore draft and my sea draft were finished at RNAS Culdrose I was happy because this meant I was now free to move further afield, to seek out new adventures and see and learn new things. I then headed for HMS Drake where I worked alongside some brilliant submarinas for my shore draft. I remember at that time, the most fun I had was at meal times when a group of us would all sit together and have a go at each other during our meals. It was quite entertaining and full of fun. They were; Earl, Nick, and a friend whom we called Candy, it was brilliant. My next stop was HMS Excellent where I worked with the Royal Naval Forward Logistic Site (RNFLS) which was a very glamorous draft where I had to travel overseas to set up temporary logistics teams whenever there was a vital need for this to ensure the survival of the force.

I was on the RNFLS draft when I along with a small team flew to the Eastern Mediterranean country of Cyprus which is south of Turkey and west of Syria and Lebanon, to set up an essential logistic site. Cyprus is a popular tourist and an advanced high income destination with a very high human development index. We went directly to the sovereign military base of Akrotiri. As soon as we arrived at the base I could sense an old Caribbean feel to it. It was the way the older buildings were constructed with concrete made from cement, as opposed to hard blocks I presume, and these buildings have verandas to the front of them, and the fact that everyone seemed so warm and friendly to each other. Also, of course was the fact that the base was a community within itself which might be the reason behind the well developed, favourable social infrastructure which I experienced. The weather was quite similar to that of the Caribbean's, it was pleasant and only got a bit fresh first thing in the morning, when it rained and late evening.

It was late afternoon when we all finished for the day and decided to go to a restaurant for a nice meal and a drink. We sat out in the evening sun on the terrace of a glass fronted restaurant with glamorous waiters and waitresses moving about in a swift and alert fashion. We ordered three course dishes as we planned our events for the following day's work at the end we had a drink and strolled along the beautiful white sandy beach. We went shopping for souvenirs the day before we flew back to England and I was so unhappy at this stage in my marriage that I did not buy any gifts for Roger but as usual I got something special for my little one, which by that time I was in the habit of buying t-shirts with the names of the country I visited printed on the front.

The next country I went to was Singapore which is situated next door to Malaysia to its north, has the world's fourth leading financial centres, has one of the busiest ports in the world and has the best quality of life in the Asian community. It was just a team of two of us (Wayne and myself) who went on this trip and once we arrived in Singapore we had to stay overnight in a luxurious five star hotel (not that I can imagine Singapore having anything less than five star hotels) in order to await the Edinburgh, the ship, we were meant to support in achieving its objectives while in that port.

The flight from Heathrow to Singapore lasted more than thirteen hours and we had to exchange in Doha. It was Qatar airline and the air stewardesses were very hospitable, the food was delicious and everything was sterile, even your hands and faces particularly, on the second half of the flight from Doha to Singapore. From the moment we arrived in Singapore we could tell from the feel of it that it was not a poor country. When we departed the plane at the airport people of every race, especially Asians, could be seen busying about either getting ready to board flights, getting off flights or waiting at the other end for someone who was arriving.

We collected our bags and were ourselves collected at the airport's main entrance and that is when we realized it was raining. Rain washed all about the transit van which we sat in talking with this young man about out trip and our plans to meet the ship in the dock yard the next day. Little did we know at the time that he was an officer, only second in command to the captain on the same ship we would be heading for the next day. What surprised us was his age, for he was very young, only twenty-one if my memory serves me right, but he was very nice and he told us that he would look out for us once we boarded the ship. There were other people from the Navy who were boarding the ship as well but we did not know them, nevertheless, we all had pleasant and even jovial conversations.

Each time I would pop my head up to glance through the window I would be greeted with well kept areas planted with flowers or rich vegetation. It was beautiful. We finally arrived at the Copthorne hotel which is truly luxurious with excellent service and delicious food. I had a great time soaking in the bath that night and watching people going to and coming from their night out at various hours from my transparent glass fronted room. Everything in my room was so shiny and pretty and my bed was so comfortable I could have slept-in all day after such a long flight but no such luck was afforded as I had to be up early the next day.

We got to the dock yard first thing and waited a while before the ship came into view, after the ceremony of docking the ship was over; we (Wayne and I) along with the many others who were also waiting went on board to fulfil our true mission. Whenever I was not busy working on board I would go shopping, sometimes with Wayne and at other times with other colleagues from the ship, in Singapore high streets. Shopping is all I wanted to do in Singapore because of its atmosphere. There is so much to buy and there seemed to be such good quality of everything and reasonable bargain. There were times when we (Chaz, Laura, Pam and I) went to the zoo or for a nice meal but I just felt like I was missing out when I was not shopping. On the last day I spent in Singapore, as I walked through the busy streets among crowds of people going about their business, I felt this strange sensation and I knew that this was not the last I was seeing of Singapore. I knew that one day I would take my family there for a glorious holiday so they can walk through the streets just like I did.

My final sea draft was to HMS York and my final voyage was to Jersey, which is an island within the Channel Islands. Jersey is a British crown dependency off the coast of Normandy, which is not a part of the United Kingdom though the United Kingdom is responsible for its defence. Jersey is a beautiful tiny island full of life and activities especially at night. Everyone always seemed to be out because of the hip and very modern looking restaurants, club and pubs with their upbeat music were always open until late in Jersey. It was a bright and sunny day when the ship docked in Jersey and everyone on the island, men, women, boys and girls came to visit the ship and have a general look around on board, which was very educational and informative for them. I was one of a handful of naval personnel greeting the visitors, having a good chat with most of them and telling them about the logistics branch. There were priceless, glorious military souvenirs too which all the visitors wanted to take with them.

Many of the curious, young, vibrant faces were already planning to join the military, as their parents happily informed us. So curious and excited they were that some of the presentations and dramatizations had to be done twice. By the end of the day we all got dolled up and had taken over the entire island with our merrymaking. Everyone on the island knew we were there amongst them, in their pubs, clubs and restaurants and they all welcomed us and made us feel right at home, it was magical. It was always a big group of us out and that night was no different. A friend of mine named Terry and myself were on the dance floor mashing it up as Lady Gaga's voice could be heard above the merriment and excitement singing "poker face", after that it was Tinchy Strinder's "number one", Sean Paul's, "so fine", then they played "kiss me through the phone" by Soulja Boy and many more big hits. For a minute I thought I was having a night out in Jamaica. It was a shame when the club closed and our night out was over because without a doubt we had thoroughly enjoyed our night out.

The next day I was feeling a bit sick and remembered that I had missed my menses. I was a bit concerned as I took a pregnancy test and the result confirmed my earlier suspicions. I then went to the sick bay (the medical staff on board) and saw the Petty Officer who started the procedure for me to abandon ship. I had to leave the ship in a rush as they were just about to sail. I got a flight back to England where I was drafted to Portsmouth initially and then later on, to the Armed Forces Careers Office (AFCO) in Manchester because of my condition. Furthermore my personal life was going to shreds as I was also going through my divorce and already had a young child caring for. By that time it was clear that I wouldn't be able to go back to work in the Navy because I would soon have two children to care for without the help of a partner.

By the end of my lengthy reminiscence into my Navy days George and I had eaten all the food that we had set out on the blanket at the beginning of our picnic and he was lying on his back now just looking up at me with previously excited countenance which now looked as if he was having information overload. The sun had disappeared from the sky and it was now looking as if the rain was on its way. I decided it was time I give it up and take a rest and George probably picked up on what I was thinking as he gently patted my back and said "Marge, that was a full seven pack of years you have had in the Navy!" And we both looked at each other and laughed a knowing laugh, because he remembered what I told him in a very private conversation just between the two of us about "Freddy". A male chauvinist hypocrite who left the Navy several years earlier and isn't even worth mentioning. "We have to remember to always highlight the good in everything," he said and my heart dropped. I marvelled at how easily he understood my every situation and how intensely he empathized with me, even in those situations that were most awkward. I felt such deep feelings for him. A part of me felt sure that I had known him for years; maybe in another lifetime.

A MOTHER'S AWAKENING

George and I were at a Barbeque which I had dressed casually for and was now thanking my lucky stars because the day, though it started off rather bleak and wet had turned out to be sunny and dry. I was saying a silent prayer now, thanking the Lord for this wonderful man beside me and all these sunny days to go with it. I couldn't have been happier but I knew there was something I had to share with George. Our bodies were almost touching as we sat next to each other and ate our chicken quietly. We were getting very good at shutting out large crowds of people around us in order to feel closer to and more at ease with each other. George was wearing a black sleeveless Nike silk shirt which made his toned muscles obvious and a pair of Bench jeans which also showed off his tight buttocks and stomach.

I was at the gym three times a week now so I was looking much more in shape than when I first met George, only, he doesn't know how out of shape I was because I always made sure I hid it well. I looked at his face and I knew without a doubt that he was the most handsome man I had ever seen. He had perfect skin and his height and physique made me feel secure in his presence. He was so level headed, sweet and loving that I started to think of him as 'the perfect man'. I was positive no one had it as good as me, in terms of being with a man who was outstanding company. I even impressed myself. I felt so proud as if I had achieved a great feat. My only worry now which was becoming a constant worry, was, if he would stay with me after learning what I was about to download on him but I couldn't not tell him, I loved him too much to lie.

Furthermore, it was not in me to lie, I always had to tell the truth. I took his hand and squeeze it and he watched me closely wondering what I was up to. "You know," I said, "I've got something that I have to share with you." And I could tell he knew based on my facial expression how serious the matter was. I began by telling him how much I loved Melissa and what she means to me. "I would give my life for them both, you know that." I said, and I almost forgot that I was still clinging onto his had and only realized I was, because he squeezed my hand gently and said. "I know those children are precious to you Marge, they are adorable and even I myself am becoming real fund of them."

I was so grateful to him for always making it so easy for me to be with him and for me to share with him. It reminded me of how a lot of females, like myself often say that men are not good communicators but it was different with him. I had a lot of preconceptions about men but he has proved me wrong in so many ways. With him I was glad to be proven wrong. He was truly a blessing. I looked deep into his eyes and he in mine and I knew I had to be bold "I had postpartum psychosis as a result of my last pregnancy." I told him and he kept hold of my hand and my gaze into his eyes and said, "What do you mean Marge, could you please explain?" I felt a shiver run through my body as I wondered where to start but I knew I was doing the right thing. I started off with an even tone and a neutral expression on my face. "Let me explain." I said.

Well, shortly before I became pregnant I bought a house which I am paying mortgage for. By the time I became pregnant I was already divorcing Roger and giving up my job in the navy in order to care for my children. I guess I didn't realize how much stress I was putting myself under by making every possible change in my life all at once. You see, I was giving up everything I was used to, my job for seven years, my husband, my old address in the south in order to move into the house I had bought and even the size family I was used to because with the birth of my new child I no longer had one child to cope with which I was used to doing now having done it for nine years prior to this, I would be giving birth to a second child. Even my furniture changed as previously I was using Navy furniture but now I had bought my own furniture. We had moved away from all our friends and Rosie had to change school so we were making an entirely new beginning overall. The icing on the cake was my very difficult and nerve wrecking labour during childbirth. The baby was due on the 30th December but when the baby didn't budge labour was induced two weeks after, on the very last day she was allowed to stay inside me.

I don't know if it was the lack of support during the nine months of my pregnancy while at the same time going through turmoil in other areas of my life or if it was just the labour itself or both, but the excruciating pain I felt during labour can never be compared to any other and was more than enough to drive any human being ballistic. I remember how excited I was about my little one throughout the pregnancy. The bulge in my stomach is the only thing that kept me going during those very difficult, lonely and sad months. I would go to and from work feeling like a zombie because my whole world had turned upside down around me. I was plagued with morning sickness as well and even when I wasn't being sick I felt like I was going to be sick to my stomach. My worst times were first thing in the morning, after each meal and at night.

There were days when I awoke as early as 0200 after finding it hard to fall asleep the night before anyway and not be able to go back to sleep until 0600 or 0700 and this was just too close to the time for me to start out for work so I was always restless. There were days when, because of my very strange sleeping patterns coupled with sickness I would just not be able to get out of bed.

By the time I took my small green suitcase packed with proper night dresses and gowns, birthing dresses, bed slippers, toiletries, a suit of clothes to wear home, couple of suits of clothes for the new born, towels, under-wears, maternity napkins and the baby car seat on top. I was massive in size and completely worn out by my pregnancy. Nevertheless, I was totally anxious to see the baby and was happy that this day had arrived. I was in labour before I knew what had hit me and was already in a lot of pain from about 1300 at the very beginning. It was about 0900 when I was induced and so comfortable was the little one inside me that I still managed to start labour in the afternoon.

As soon as labour began I was given gas and air which only seemed to make the pain worse and because I didn't have much of a choice I just continued on it hoping that it would eventually ease the pain. I had requested TENS as a form of pain relief during labour but the hospital did not have any in stock and looking back, I am very doubtful it would have worked for me anyway. I was told that I wouldn't be given epidural which I felt should have been reconsidered since I wasn't responding very well to the gas and air.

It went on like this for hours and what made my situation even worse was the fact that my ex-husband came to visit me in the hospital and stood there watching me in labour. As soon as I saw him that afternoon all the anger and hurt during our marriage and subsequent divorce kept flooding back as though it was yesterday and this was very upsetting. The trauma from the divorce was still fresh in my mind anyway because it was only two months now that the divorce had become final. The fact that I was already having a difficult labour didn't help. I could have torn my hair out. He was the very last person I wanted to see at that time and each time I wanted to urinate, which was often, I had to ask him to leave the room, which he did unwillingly and in his own time.

I remember at one point my phone was ringing and I was in so much pain and agony, I couldn't answer it and just wanted the damn thing to stop, but no, he was not having it, "Marge," he said, "Answer your phone! Why are you not answering your phone?" Even though I was making animal noises by this point the only thing that seemed to trouble him in the least was the fact that I wasn't answering my phone. It was a time when he confirmed to me that I was not one bit too hasty in my decision to divorce him and that we belong to two different planets. I asked the staff to remove him from my room which they did grudgingly since I imagine he told them he was my husband. I wanted to choke on my puke. He then sat outside and waited for me to deliver him a baby. I was so furious that I couldn't sort him out but I was in too much pain to take him on.

About 2330 they informed me that they had to remove me to the labour ward and it was alright with me, only I couldn't get up because the pain was so bad that even when I wiggled my big toe in the slightest the pain was catastrophic. They eventually offered me a wheel chair and I looked at the chair for several minutes but couldn't bring myself to climbing into it for fear of the pain which would go with it from the moment I shift my body until the moment I get into bed again in the labour ward. I started feeling so pathetic having the staff stand around waiting for me just to shift from the bed to the chair that I just gave up and decided to take the pain head on. I literally ran from the bed to the chair which they had placed right in front of the bed and while they wheeled me down the long corridor I kept begging them to hurry. When they finally got next to the bed in the labour ward I decided to brave it again and just dashed from the chair onto the bed without giving it much thought.

They checked me again and announced that the baby was 4 cm dilated and told me that I had a lot of work to do. I was in even more pain now so I asked the staff again for epidural, who were sitting directly in front of me looking into my vagina as though they were in the cinema watching a cool film, and they just repeated what they said earlier, "no, we are not going to be able to give you epidural mam." It infuriated me and at that moment I felt so desperate. I truly thought that the baby and I were going to die because I just couldn't bear the pain anymore and I had to be dilated another six centimetres more before the baby would come.

There was no way in heaven or hell I was going to be able to bear the pain I had already bore for the same duration plus half that time. In fact I felt I wasn't even able to bear the pain for another minute. I had no one to give me support and to encourage me at all. I only had myself to lean on. "I am going to die." I told the staff, a female doctor and her nurse, but they just looked past me as though they heard nothing. I decided that I was going to have to help myself or end up in the morgue, both my unborn child and I.

I looked up at the clock on the wall above and it read 2335. At that time the large double doors opened up to the small private room where I lay in the only bed within the room and I looked up just in time to see Roger being escorted into the room but I couldn't object at that point because of the deadly, painful contractions which were like one big constant pain, pain mixed with anger and disgust. I knew I couldn't let him stay otherwise the morgue wasn't going to miss us. He was now sitting on an armchair looking directly at my private bits without any emotions.

It was several months before the divorce was finalized that we were separated and living apart because during our last months together he did everything to provoke and frustrate me to the point where I felt the baby was in danger. I wasn't coping at all with him around and my situation was already problematic without him adding to it. I boldly decided I was going to push the baby out ready or not because I was going to die otherwise, and the baby as well because I just couldn't bear it anymore but I couldn't bring myself to deal with the situation and do what was crucial in the moment in Roger's presence. "Can you please ask him to go?" I said, knowing that I would have to endure yet another argument with Roger had I asked him directly. I couldn't handle an argument, especially not with Roger in my state. "Are you sure you want him to go mam?" the doctor asked and I said, "Yes," in a loud voice, just about losing patience with her. I was aware of her asking him to leave and him insisting that he being there was the best thing for me and so it went for a good three minutes until he finally put his knap sack on his back and left unwillingly.

As soon as he was out the door I pushed way down in my bottom with all my might and nothing happened. I knew I was running out of time and I pushed with all the force of my being, long and hard and still nothing. "I am not going to give up, I have to get the baby out," I thought, but if I was going to beat death and survive this ordeal it had to be done now. "It isn't even time yet for me to push," I thought, " but I've got to do this right now," I pushed with all the strength I never knew I had in me and the two staff jumped from their seats and shouted in disbelief, "the baby is coming." Not even I myself could believe it as I continued to push strenuously and felt the baby literally shoving its way out of my vagina.

The staff grabbed the baby and announced in unison that it was a girl. They then cut the umbilical cord and she did not cry. They did not seem bothered by this but I asked them why the baby wasn't crying a couple of times and when I didn't get much of a response I insisted that something was wrong and at that point they said they would get the paediatrician to have a look at her, which they did a couple minutes after. He explained that because the baby came out so fast she didn't get a chance to prepare herself to breath naturally and this is why she did not cry when she first came out. She was crying now and it sounded a bit painful for her and the paediatrician told me that it would be a bit painful for her whenever she cried for a while so I should try to keep her crying at a minimum.

I felt a bit guilty for causing this complication for her but I also knew I did my best in the circumstances. They then weighed her, wrapped her in a blanket and immediately after that, put her to suckle on my right breast where we had skin to skin first contact. I looked down at my little bundle in disbelief as she sucked forcefully on my tender breast which was full of colostrum. The staff then went over slowly in a dream like way what had happened in the last few minutes. They kept congratulating me for getting the baby out while I was only 4cm dilated saying they had never seen anything like it before. "You were only 4 cm dilated and yet you pushed the baby out. That is very good Mrs. McFarlane. And here we were thinking it was going to be a difficult one! Eight pounds and ten ounces she weighs and she is very tall as well." Said the doctor. I was puzzled by that bit of news because in my family it was unheard of for a newborn to weigh that much. I looked down at her sparkling bright eyes staring up at me and marvelled at how much she looked like her father. I was so happy that we were both alive and well and I said a silent prayer of thanks. The gynaecologist came in and checked me shortly after while my little one slept in her cot. She gave me a couple of stitches and told me I was fine.

I then went for a bath, after which we were both escorted off the labour ward and onto the postnatal ward where other mothers were with their babies and the staff there kept repeating how beautiful my baby was. I fed her again and laid her down to sleep in a tiny, transparent cot which was placed next to my bed. It must have been about 0300 when I fell asleep myself and didn't even realize I had until I was awoken the next morning by my baby's distinctive crying. From then on it was as though I hadn't recovered from the whole experience of labour the previous night. I was overwhelmingly tired and couldn't seem to get enough sleep, but the baby, though she was a good baby and didn't cry unless she needed changing or feeding, I always felt as though I was spending all my time tending to her when in fact half the time I was just trying to recover from my fatigue. Also, it took me a while to realize I was hardly eating anything.

A few days after, I felt as though my baby's father was able to see me in my house and was interfering with how I was caring for her. I was livid. My sister April and her partner Tyrone came from their home in New York to visit us when the baby was a week old but so engulfed I was in the whole ordeal that they left prematurely. April didn't understand what I was going through and I myself had no idea what was happening with me. Again I felt I had no one to turn to.

I spoke to the relevant authorities who ensured that I was treated for my condition in the healthy environs of Laureate house mother and baby unit. It wasn't until I went into the hospital and contacted my family in Jamaica that April realized what I was going through and we were able to mend things between us. I and my baby were treated like guests in an all inclusive hotel for the full length of our stay.

After six weeks I was well again and was more than happy to go home and take my life back. I found that throughout the duration of my illness that each individual who was involved with my case, in whatever capacity, had my best interest at heart and carried out his or her job brilliantly. I will always be indebted to them.

My hand was feeling numb now as George continually squeezed it throughout my detailed explanation of my ordeal and at the end he collected me in his arms and held me close to him. I felt so safe and protected from harm. "Don't worry sweetheart," he said, "I'm here for you." "Oh George," I said as I buried my head in his chest, tears ran down my face and he just stood there patting at my back and rocking me softly in his arms. I felt so emotional and I think it's because I had relived a very bitter time in my life. "He is staying," I told myself happily as he released me after holding me in his arms for about five minutes and asked me tenderly if I wanted us to get some more chicken and I happily said, "Yes."

MY PRECIOUS GIRLS

The girls were having a brilliant time at their aunt Althea's and uncle Jeff's. They were taken to the beach regularly where they had festival and fish while they listened and danced to the groovy sound systems as evening drew near. Here it was more about blending in with and enjoying the rich culture of the massive beach so very little time was wasted in the water. It was common practise for everyone to take a quick dip in the clear, blue sea then they would wrap their towels about them on their way to checking out the wide variety of fish for sale in any of a number of food huts along the water's edge. At other times they were taken to the movies where they would watch the latest children's film out, or for a meal at McDonald's, Kentucky Fried Chicken's (KFC) or Burger King's. There were days when they would stay at the shop and watch their aunt and uncle intriguingly, as they work all day.

Their aunt who is petite, beautiful and fashionable usually checks at the till while their uncle who is tall and strapping goes out every morning to purchase their daily stock of grocery and stores them away then last thing in the evenings he would ensure that the shop is fully stocked for the next day. This the girls as well as their cousins found fascinating and were too busy snacking on a wide variety of snacks for a greater part of the day anyway so they never had time to get bored while they were at the shop.

One Sunday while the girls were still at aunt Althea's and uncle Jeff's their aunt April and uncle Tyrone contacted them on web cam via the internet from America to see how they were enjoying their visit to Jamaica. Rosie examined her aunt April's features closely as her face appeared on the computer screen while she said hello. It had been a while since she had last seen her aunt. "She is quite beautiful and youthful looking as well," she thought. Rosie told her aunt April and uncle Tyrone, her partner, all about the time they spent in Montego Bay, Old Harbour and about what they were getting up to, now that they were in Greater Portmore. "So, where have you enjoyed the most?" asked uncle Tyrone and Rosie thought for a bit and then answered, "Well, we have enjoyed the time we have spent with each of our aunts and uncles equally though each of them for different reasons." She then went on to explain in detail and they could see that both she and little Melissa were having a great time from what she had said and from the little they could see of them through the web cam.

She knew it was good for them because while Melissa was meeting her maternal grandmother, aunts, uncles and cousins for the first time, Rosie hadn't seen them for a long time and was losing touch with her roots fast. "Do you miss your mom?" April asked. "Yes, we do," Rosie answered, "but I wish she didn't have to work so hard and could have taken the time out to be here enjoying herself with us." "Oh, she is so grown up." April thought to herself admiringly but before she could say anything else her three boys (Norman, Stanley and Jack) barged in and took over the conversation.

They all wanted to know what had changed in Jamaica since they were last there, which was in January 2008 for the unfortunately, sad and tearful event of their Aunt Bianca's funeral. Also, they all wanted to hear about the new cousins they had that they hadn't met in person yet. They talked at great lengths and were more than satisfied that they were brought up to date in the matter by the time their parents informed them they had to go. They quickly said good bye to Rosie and of course to Melissa as she babbled back to them, before they closed off.

Before long it was time for the girls to visit with yet another of their aunts, this time it was Aunt Vicky's turn and she was happy to see them. She collected them in her arms as they ran out into the front to greet her as soon as they heard her car pull up. The girls were a bit tearful to leave their aunt Althea's and Uncle Jeff's but as soon as the car got on the highway they were peering through the windows trying to figure out where they were headed. They kept up a steady conversation with their aunt Vicky who was very patient with them and answered all their questions. She was a school teacher by profession so she was used to dealing with children and their curious nature.

When she arrived in Spanish Town, she quickly stopped in at her daughter's Trudy who has recently married to Nick whom she met while they were at university together. Rosie and Trudy were very happy to see each other as they too could remember a time in the past when they were very close to each other. They had bonded well, almost like sisters, when Rosie was very young. At the end of their short visit to Trudy's with promises that they would see each other again in the next few days their aunt Vicky left with the girls for her place. By the time they got to Aunt Vicky's it was late evening and she barely had enough time to prepare stir fried chicken and vegetables with pasta. The girls ate their meal happily, were seen to their bath and to bed where they had a long and restful night.

The next morning they were awaken to the smell of eggs, bacon, sausages and toast and for a moment they thought they were back with their mom. They both woke up at the same time calling for their mom and came out of the bedroom following the smell of the food into the kitchen where they found their aunt Vicky who hugged them and comforted them until they calmed down enough to sit and have their breakfast at the breakfast bar. "I thought it was mom cooking you know." Said Rosie, as she bit into her large sandwich, which she made with everything on her plate. "It didn't make sense that we would suddenly be where mom was but it just smelt and felt like mom was here." She continued. "I know darling, don't worry, when you talk to your mom just before bedtime as usual you can tell her all about it, but don't let her worry too much because she is trying very hard to find a job right now." Said Aunt Vicky and Rosie replied, "Alright aunt Vicky," In agreement.

Later on that day Aunt Vicky took the girls to meet the class that she teaches at school. The children were the same age as Rosie and they were so happy to see their aunt Vicky, they started to complain to her about the substitute teacher who was teaching them until she returned and were very unhappy to see their teacher whom they had from the previous year and felt so close to, leave, though it was only for a few days. Though they were happy to meet Rosie and Melissa they were a bit jealous of them as well so they were more than glad to see them go. For the rest of the time at aunt Vicky's, Rosie and Melissa were taken to the movies and out for meals. Most of the time was used though to go through lessons with Rosie to ensure she stayed on top of things she might be missing out on at school, while Melissa played with her toys and watched television or just took her morning or afternoon naps. At times the girls would be taken to Trudy's and Nick's as promised where they would play computer games and just hang out.

When it was time for them to leave Spanish Town and head for

Kingston the girls realized that it was getting harder and harder to break away from one set of aunts and uncles to move on to their visit with the next set but Rosie knew this time they would be visiting their grandmother. She also knew how much she wanted to see her grandmother whom she loved dearly. In fact she was very eager to see her and the rest of her cousins in Kingston. She knew how much her grandmother missed her too and that she would be waiting and preparing tirelessly for their visit. She found that it didn't matter where she went to in Jamaica, she couldn't wait to get back to Kingston.

The girls were dropped off by their aunt Vicky at about noon and immediately went in search of their grandmother. It wasn't long before they found her tucked away in her bedroom where she was lying across her bed awaiting their arrival but she was so tired after her spring cleaning, in preparation for the girls visit, she fell asleep while waiting. They noticed that the house was even neater than usual and Rosie wondered how much time she spent getting it that way. As soon as she saw them she bundled them up in her arms and held them there until Rosie shifted and then she sat them down to a large meal. She had made boiled firmly ripen plantains and salt fish and a host of puddings, pies and cakes she had spent hours baking especially for the girls.

Later, their aunt Carla, their uncle Phillip and Carla's three children and her granddaughter Laurie, joined the girls and their grandmother for their evening meal. Rosie enjoyed spending time with Kimani and Henry, both of whom she got along well with while she lived in Jamaica. They had a long discussion all evening about school, church and electronic games, such as, the Wii console, Xbox 360, Play station 3, DS 3D, DSI and PSP while Melissa and Laurie made the most of each other, chasing each other around the room and screaming with laughter. Their aunt Carla helped their grandmother with the meal and after a while their uncle who is a Rastafarian allowed the girls to touch his long locks and was more than happy to answer Rosie's questions about the Rastafarian faith. As he answered her bombardment of questions she noticed that he was very gentle and sincere and she was glad that she had a Rastafarian in her family so that she could learn so much about this previously unusual religion she has been noticing for a while now.

When the meal was ready their aunt Carla called everyone to the table as their grandmother took her seat at the head of the table. The delicious yam, bananas, dumplings, potatoes and baked chicken which was laid out on the table as everyone sat down to eat disappeared in no time as everyone helped themselves. The children picked up from where they left off earlier and were engulfed in their conversation about games while the adults spoke quietly about how different the girls were from their mother and how adorable they were. Shortly after they all left it was the girls' bedtime so their grandmother gave them a warm hug each and saw them off to bed.

The next day it was Aunt Amanda's turn to take the girls for a day out and she took her three children and two grand children along. The girls' grandmother went along with them as well. Their aunt Amanda hired a transit van which took them on their way to the Guardman's Serenity Fishing and Wildlife Sanctuary first thing in the morning. Everyone got their turn on a tractor ride through mango orchards and vegetable plots when they first arrived, which they enjoyed very much. They then had a visit to the animal collection, with exotic birds and a petting zoo which they couldn't get enough of.

Everyone marvelled at the animals especially the younger children who were seeing some of the animals for the very first time. They walked from one end of the zoo to the other excitedly as they discussed the different animals on show. Rosie spent most of her time holding hands with her older cousin Katie, whom she gets on very well with while their grandmother pushed Melissa in her push chair. When they got to the last set of animals, some colourful and very unusual German parrots the children insisted that they go around again as they hadn't had enough. They finally break for lunch eventually and ate their curried goat, stew chicken or fried chicken and rice and peas while they swayed to the rhythms of reggae music which played in the background.

Their late aunt Bianca's daughters Petula who has an amazing voice and sings at every family event bringing everyone to tears and Keisha a stern school teacher, took them down town to the national art gallery which contain some real treasures the following morning. Petula and Keisha had three children each of their own who they took along to the museum as well. The best known artists represented at the gallery are Edna Manley who was an accomplished artist and wife of the former Prime Minister, Norman Manley and Kapo, whose religious images have received a lot of attention. Rosie, as did the other older children, examined each work of art closely and inquisitively and learnt a lot about art by the end of the tour while Melissa enjoyed looking at the colourful pieces and scampering in the open spaces.

"Hello?" I answered with a questioning voice, wondering who it might be. "Don't worry dear, it's only me, did I catch you at a bad time?" asked my mother in a caring voice. "No mom, it's ok, I just finished my lunch and was just seeing to some cleaning, that's all." I told her. "Well dear, I know you have been in touch with the girls every day and you are well up to date with what's happening with them but I've been wanting to have a talk with you for the last two days but my hands have been full with them but not to worry. They are being taken to the art gallery this morning by Petula and Keisha so it gives me a chance to catch up with you," explained my mother. "Oh, that's great, the children will love visiting the art gallery especially Rosie who is into art so much, there isn't a time when she is ever out of a painting set and a sketch pad and Melissa will love the bright colours and the open spaces where she can move about freely." I responded.

"Talking about Melissa, she is a beautiful little girl isn't she? But she is a lot like her father, pretty much like Rosie is, I imagine because she is nothing like you," mom said. "I am glad you can finally see it for yourself mom because it's not as clear to you until you can see it for yourself," I said. "Well dear, all I can say is that you have been through a lot with her but when I look at her and bundle her up in my arms I think of you and my heart rejoice that you are back on your feet but I also have to say that she is worth the trouble," said mom sincerely. "Don't worry mom, I know she is, it's ok. In fact, you know what has been happening a lot mom? Whenever I take the kids shopping with me a lot of people ask me why I don't enter Melissa in the Bounty Baby Competition because of her appearance," I said proudly. "That's great sweetheart, I agree, she is a real little stunner and Rosie as well. It's funny how things work out.

Anyone would have thought you'd have more of a difficult time giving birth to your first child and not the ones that follow so much, isn't it?" She said questioningly. "But mom, I did have a hard time giving birth to Rosie as well you know. You might have forgotten all the details because it was roughly ten years ago but the staff at the hospital who cared for me leading up to my labour with Rosie, their behaviour was inflammatory. I remember it like it was yesterday. I had to be induced on the very last day for Rosie as well because the due date had passed uneventfully. I had a private gynaecologist whom I saw very often and who was also there at Rosie's birth and there were some brilliant midwives as well who did their best under the circumstances but it was the hours leading up to the birth that was catastrophic.

I was induced about 0700 and my contractions started at about 1100. The pain was excruciating so I was crying each time I had a contraction but the staff on the ward, particularly this nurse who was from Zimbabwe, told me that I should stop my crying because I was disturbing others on the ward. When I could not grant their wish they began to get upset with me and when my contractions became more regular and I was removed to this special room where I was put by myself, where I was meant to wait until the very first sign of labour my cries for help were ignored.

Later when I was finally checked the male nurse who checked me said he was not aware of my fast progress and immediately rushed me into the labour ward in alarm. By the time they put me on this ridiculous table with my feet up in stirrups on either side, because I was not informed that I should not push the baby out until I am told to when I feel the contractions, I was pushing right throughout so the baby was coming fast. By that time the caring midwives in the labour ward were asking me to try to hold the baby in and complaining that they were not ready while they rushed about trying to get their gear in place.

Without further warning the baby popped right out and was only saved by one of the midwives who was passing and looking up my rear end by chance that second otherwise who knows what would have happened to my baby. At that very minute when the midwife caught my baby my gynaecologist walked in and was in shock at what almost happened. 'Shock' does not even begin to explain how I felt about the whole ordeal but the happiest moment of my life was when I held my newborn for the first time." I paused and gave mom a chance to comment. "It was almost a tragic end you know dear, the hospital would have been in a lot of trouble for that if that midwife, God bless her soul, didn't save the day," said mom. "I know mom. I'm just grateful that she has come this far." I said. "I know. I can't get over how much she has grown and matured. "She must be doing very well at school, she is so intelligent," said mom. "Yes, I'm pleased with her progress. She had to change school a lot when I was in the Navy and she went to three different schools in the South of England before we finally got settled here.

I can still remember the first school she went to in England. It was in Cornwall, she was four and her lovely brilliant teacher was the wife of our reverend at church. A parent told me that she saw a confrontation between Rosie and the other children in her class. The children all circled around Rosie and wouldn't let her through, shouting 'dragon' at her. I was heart broken when I heard and I know that what they did was wrong but what I also know is that Rosie has a strong personality and sometimes even adults feel threatened by her strong presence. I look at her and I see right in front of me a candidate for barrister-ship though I have to admit that at times she is a bit cheeky as well but that will go in time. She did very well at all the schools she has attended especially that brilliant school in Gosport. I don't think the people in that community realize the full strength of that school which is a shame because in my mind it is just as good as the private school she is used to attending whenever she had to be back in Jamaica for any length of time.

The school she attends today is a very good school as well which sees her getting through to go to my first choice high school for her, which is an accomplishment I'm grateful to them for helping her achieve." I explained. "That's very good dear." My mom said. "Mom, even her friendships were affected by our constant moving. For her birthday parties it was mostly my friends who attended to support and cheer her up because we moved about so much it was hard for her to keep up with her friendships because she was always seen as the new girl at school which took a little time to wear off but she will be fine now. She has been so strong all these years," I said. "Your little one seems to be following in Rosie's foot-steps you know. She imitates everything Rosie does which is good because Rosie is doing so well so you have nothing to worry about," Said mom. "I've noticed mom, isn't that great? Now I feel like the hard work which I've done bringing Rosie up will be adequate for both girls," I told her. "You must be very proud of yourself. You have accomplished a lot you know and you have been very strong," said mom. "I am proud of my accomplishments." I assured her. It's a pity things didn't work out with Melissa's dad," she said. "Mom it's ok, that was a long time ago.

I've met an eligible bachelor anyway and we care about each other very much," I told her. "So, how comes you haven't told me this before? Are you hiding things from me dear?" She asked. "No mom, I've hardly told anyone about him yet. We're only dating at the moment but I have a really good feeling about him." I explained. "Great news, what does he do?" She asked. "He's a Car Salesman but he has been looking into starting his own business," I said. "What kind of business?" She asked curiously. "Well, he is looking at buying a wedding venue and catering for weddings and other events," I told her. "That is a brilliant idea." She said. "It would be even better if you could partner with him if everything works out between you two. Two heads are always better than one." She continued before I could get a word in. "Well, fingers crossed mom." I said and she closed off by saying that she had some cleaning to do herself; before the girls return so she'd better go.

CHRISTMAS

The girls had so much fun that when it was time for them to leave they were a bit resistant but they missed their mom so much and were aware of how much their mom missed them that it didn't last for long. Their belongings were packed for them by their grandmother the night before. She knew how much she would miss them, also, she was afraid that it would be a while before she would see them again but she understood that even though it didn't always show that their mom was missing them loads. She was aware of how strong her daughter was but she needed the time to build herself up so she can be even stronger for the girls. The girls were awoken at 0730 by their grandmother who got up from 0600 and made them a large breakfast and also prepared fried fish, boiled ackees and peeled sliced mangoes in a jar for them to take back with them for their mom. She remembered how much their mom loves mangoes. The girls ate their porridge, fried dumplings and callaloo quietly, except for a few babbles every now and again from Melissa.

Their bath was then seen to and then they were dressed for their trip back. It was a while before they would be picked up by the taxi but their grandmother was content knowing that they were ready for their trip. She engaged Rosie in a game of snakes and ladders while Melissa watched cartoons next to them on the large sofa in front of the television. They enjoyed their last game together and talked and laughed just like they always did while they played. Pretty soon all their maternal family living in Kingston came to say farewell. Those that were living further afield had already said goodbye to the girls as they departed their residences. Amanda arrived at the same time as the taxi and then it was time to leave.

Rosie hugged and kissed her relatives and told Kimani, Henry and Katie that she would keep in touch with them and they all held Melissa up in their hands for the last time and kissed her goodbye. They were all waving the girls goodbye as they hopped into the taxi with their aunt Amanda and their grandmother. On their way out to the airport their aunt Amanda made a quick stop where she works at the UWI Main Library and the girls were polite to all the staff, most of whom knew their mom because of her regular use of the library when she was studying and also because she worked there as Student Assistant while she studied. They enjoyed buzzing about as they took in the endless number of large shelves stacked with thousands of books of various size, shape and colour. They marvelled at the studious looking students as they studied calmly in quiet corners all about the library. She took them to see Shelly who is Rosie's father's cousin and they had a very pleasant reunion for it was a while since they had last seen each other. Shelly made the most of little Melissa and showed the girls pictures of her own little girl. Shelly made a mental note to share their visit with her with her cousin Chris, whom she knew would understand that Rosie was spending time catching up with her mother's side of the family for this brief trip.

Soon it was time for them to be on their way so they said a quick goodbye and hopped back into the taxi. Their grandmother cried hot tears which ran down her cheeks as she handed them over to the air stewardess, Pamella Stewart, and said her final goodbye. She hugged them in a tight embrace and they clung onto her in return. Both their grandmother and their aunt stood and watched as the girls left with the air stewardess. As soon as the edge wore off their final farewell they were settled in and looking forward to their long trip back to their mother. "Soon they would be back with their mom," they thought. They were happy and excited and Melissa was looking forward to Christmas because of all the gifts she knew she would be getting and the one thing she couldn't resist was going through the gifts under the Christmas tree early, trying to get permission to open them.

It was Christmas Eve and the merriment of the season could be felt in the air and be seen everywhere. The shops were filled with people doing Christmas shopping, the decorations were up and there was a cheerful mood all about. The television channels, print media and radio stations were all rudimentarily carrying Christmas programmes. George and I did our fair share of shopping and got a brand new six feet tall Christmas tree which we carefully decorated. We stocked up on snacks and sweets for the seasonal celebrations. We wrapped and laid out all of our presents under the Christmas tree days earlier.

George had picked me up at 0700 and I was for once wearing comfortable blue jeans from Next, a cream coloured sweater and ankle high medium height boots. George paced himself really well because we had an early start so we had plenty of time to get there on time in spite of the Christmas traffic being a bit bumper to bumper. I looked over at him now and he was smiling a knowing smile while focusing on the CD which was bellowing out Rihanna's "only girl in the world" song. I could see that he was priding himself and posing for me now and I admired him for looking so cool and sexy. "Boy," I thought, "If there was ever a hot boy, he is it." We arrived at the airport and pulled into the terminal and by the time we got to the information desk we were right on time.

A few minutes after the air stewardess could be seen approaching with Melissa in her push chair and Rosie by her side. They were so excited to see us and we them. I rushed up to them and grabbed Rosie, who was making her way towards us, I hugged her tightly and kissed her face as she whispered in my ear, "Mom, I missed you." "I've missed you too my darling." I said in response. I then went up to where the air stewardess was standing and swiftly swept Melissa from her push chair. She jumped with joy as she babbled her greetings to me and I marvelled at how much she seemed to have grown in such a short space of time. I was so touched by her cuteness. I held her close to me for a while and just rubbed her back then pulled her away and kissed her face, while she smiled her full faced smile and screamed with delight.

I thanked the air stewardess as she briefed me on the happenings during their flight. I strapped Melissa back into her push chair and shove her while Rosie walked by my side to where George was still standing, about ten feet from where the air stewardess stood earlier with the children. He was still looking at us with excitement written all over his face as we got closer and closer to him. We stood directly in front of him and as he examined the children closely for a minute I could tell that he was a bit nervous, meeting the girls in person now for the first time, though he had spoken to them on several occasions over the phone. George had no children of his own so this was all new to him.

He confidently stepped forward and said to Rosie who was looking up at him curiously and examining him closely, "I bet you are Rosie." As he offered his hand to her and she took it politely and said, "Yes, I am Rosie, and you are George, aren't you?" As she thought of the conversations they had on the phone. "You bet I am," he said, "I am please to finally meet you in person Rosie and of course your sister Melissa too." "Me too," she said and as soon as they released each other hand George reached down and took Melissa out of her push chair. He held her up high and she screamed happily. He then started introducing himself to her and she smiled back at him as though she understood what he was saying. In quick successions he then held her as high as he could get her up in the air and then held her down in front of him. She screamed even louder and I knew instinctively that he would be a good father to the girls. We collected their luggage and in no time we were home.

I quickly saw to the girls' bath and cooked up a meal of spaghetti bolognese which George and the girls enjoyed thoroughly. We were in the living room now watching Bratz, one of Rosie's old favourites which we were all enjoying when Rosie, eyeing the gifts under the Christmas tree asked if she could open her Christmas presents. I told her "No" firmly and was happy when she turned her interest instead to playing on her DS at the end of the movie and even invited George to play with her. I was happy that she was getting on well with George though I had no doubt that they would because I was aware of his fatherly qualities. I was also conscious of the vital need for a good father figure in the upbringing of my girls. Melissa was waltzing around the lounge exploring, as usual she had removed all the DVD's and CD's from their shelves and was now playing with the roses George had given me the day before. Whenever George gave me flowers, which was pretty often, I'd always take out a few stalks from the bunch and place them in a red vase I keep on the lounge window sill so the world could see my beautiful flowers and also George could see when my flowers were stale in case he wanted to get me a fresh bunch. I freshened her up, changed her into her little pink sleep suit and gave her a bowl of Cow and Gate milk with some flakes of cereal and she fell asleep almost instantaneously in my arms. I tucked her into her cot and switched on her night light and her monitor.

I went back downstairs and as I passed the lounge I could hear George and Rosie competing jovially in yet another game on the DS. I knew I had to pre-prepare my Christmas meals so that I wouldn't have to spend all day in the kitchen on Christmas day, missing out on all the fun. I went into the kitchen and headed straight for the fridge and took out the fresh vegetables that I needed to season my meat. I then took the turkey, ham and duck which I had removed from the freezer earlier in order that they would be defrosted in time for me to season and leave to marinade overnight which would drastically speed up the cooking process in the morning and also improve on the tastes. I quickly removed all the unwanted fat and undesirables from each meat, washed them, seasoned them with vegetables and spices and put them in containers and in the fridge to marinade until morning.

I then got out my new recipe for a delectable Christmas pudding which looked more enticing than the one I had been making for the past couple of years, found all the items in the same order as they appeared on my list and lined them out on the cupboard top next to the large baking tin. Afterwards, I returned upstairs to Rosie's bedroom where I changed her bedding and put on the pink, colourful, girly ones I'd bought only days earlier, dusted the furniture and rearranged everything on top of her dressing table and chest of drawers neatly. I did the same to my room, replacing my bedding with new silk ones I had bought. I knew I wouldn't be able to sort out Melissa's room until tomorrow and the hoovering would have to wait too because I didn't want to wake her up. The only time I was able to complete a project without being distracted is when Melissa was asleep and even Rosie at times, depending on what the project was. Finally, I went into the bathroom and gave the bath tiles a good spray and wipe with the tile cleaner, washed the bathe and the toilet and swept the floor briskly.

My work is done for tomorrow I thought as I went back downstairs to the lounge to sit and observe Rosie and George as they played the last of their games. George glanced at me as I re-entered the lounge and he empathized with me as he said, "I imagine you are tired now Marge, I'll be leaving in a minute and you get some rest, we all have an early start tomorrow." I tried to stop him rushing off and told him he could stay for as long as he wanted but it was to no avail and before long he was breezing through the front door with his coat in his hand and shouting good bye behind him.

It was about 2100 when George left and I sent Rosie up to get ready for bed. Normally she would be in bed by 2000 but whenever she was on holidays from school or on weekends I would let her stay up an hour later. She was seasoned to this now and left without argument. I could see that the yuletide season was making her excited, that and the fact that she had found herself a games playing partner in George. She always complained that she had no one to play with and was always too happy to invite all of her friends for sleep overs on the weekends and during the holidays, from school, for as far back as I can remember. I always felt a bit guilty about not having a child close to her age a long time ago, then, she wouldn't feel so lonely. I straightened up the lounge and sat down for a quick cup of tea, while I planned a mental programme for the following day.

I finally took a long shower and crawled into bed at 2145. I felt so lucky. I now had all the three most important people in my life all together with me and things were still going much better than I expected. I was very happy. For many years I felt as though I had nothing to celebrate at Christmas time so I always just go through the motion for the sake of my family, even while I was married, but now I was really anticipating tomorrow and what it would bring. I thought about the presents I had bought and went over it in my head. I had bought a set of building blocks for Melissa, which I knew she would enjoy playing with, a book on how to perform domestic chores for Rosie, which I hoped she would appreciate as she was now ten and would be eleven soon I thought it was full time she started to get around and start giving me a hand in the house, regardless of how little a help it may be and finally a set of travel cases for George.

I wondered a while what to buy him and tried to get a hint from him on many occasions and he would just constantly tell me that he didn't want me to go to any trouble for him, that I shouldn't buy him anything for Christmas, "But how could I not buy anything for the one I love at Christmas," I thought. In the end I thought if I got him something practical and not shiny and overly expensive he might not mind too much. I bought a stuffed rabbit for Melissa on Rosie's behalf and a diary for Rosie on Melissa's behalf. I also bought small gifts for George on the girls' behalf and cards for everyone and on everyone's behalf. I wondered what George had bought for the girls. His gift for Melissa was huge and heavy and Rosie's was not as big and not as heavy but was by no means less intimidating. I looked at the small box with my name written on it, the card reads "To my wonderful sweetheart, from your George" and I wondered if it was something shiny or practical. My last thought before I fell deeply into sleep was of George and what he might be doing right now, alone at home. I wondered how much longer until I could care for him so he wouldn't have to worry about his meals, clothes or his surroundings. I had such a deep love for him and wanted to be there for him at all times and I was sure he felt the same way about me and was quite fund of the girls.

It was 0600 when I got up on Christmas morning. I felt the excitement mounting as I climbed out of bed and quietly showered and dressed for the day. I didn't want to over dress for the day but at the same time I didn't want to under-dress because even though we would be spending the day at home having a pretty traditional Christmas I knew it was a day that would be remembered for a long time to come and I didn't want to be remembered as frumpy looking and unattractive. I had this very provocative bronze coloured dress which my sister April sent me from America and I knew I had to get it on. I put on some makeup and a two inch heel shoes which go very well with the dress. I decided to put my hair up for a change and realized that George had never seen me with my hair up, I held it up to the very core of my head and tied it up with a bubble and it fell seductively all about the top of my head including my forehead.

I stepped swiftly down the stairs, headed straight for the fridge in the kitchen and took the meat I had put to marinade the night before on the kitchen counter. I then checked each of them to see if they might need more spice and when I was satisfied with them, stick them all in the oven. I put my white apron on which I knew would protect my clothes from getting soiled. I then quickly rubbed up the ingredients for the Christmas pudding and when everything was mixed to a thick, rich, creamy paste I shifted it into the oven as well. I set the table with the new red and white set of table cloth, cloth table mats, napkins, various sizes of dinner plates and drinking glasses and took my sterling silver cutlery which I bought and save for special occasions out of the cupboard. I took a couple baby potatoes out of the fridge, washed them and put them in the pyrex dish which had the duck in it. I took the mince pies and placed them in a decorative display dish and put them back in the fridge until later, likewise the cheese cake and later I would do the same with the Brussels sprouts, I had washed them and put them in a small sauce pan which I would boil on the cooker in good time.

I set on the large dutchy pot that Samantha had bought for me from London, while I was in the Navy when I lived in Plymouth, and took out a pack of kidney beans which I measured out a cup full of and washed and placed in the pot to boil. I then measured out three cups of rice which I would wash and add later to the beans and took a tin of Jamaican made coconut milk from the cupboard which I got along with other popular Jamaican produce from my local Tesco; I was more than pleased with this. I put my scallion and salt aside to cook with my rice and beans. I then set a saucepan with oatmeal to boil for breakfast, checked on the ham which looked like it would be ready soon and put a couple slices of bread in a bowl which I planned to toast as soon as the girls were up, dressed and ready for the day. I was priding myself for being able to get so much done while the girls were still sleeping.

I turned down the burners of the cooker and went upstairs to run the girls' bath but before I was finished I heard Melissa babbling and a moment later Rosie walked into the bathroom saying cheerfully, "Happy Christmas mom." I hugged her and kissed her smiling face and told her happy Christmas in return. "Can I open my presents mom?" she asked and I told her that we would open them in good time as a family when everyone was seated in the lounge after our main meal. I then added, strawberry scented bubbles, their favourite to the bath, let it run for a bit longer and asked Rosie to climb in, got Melissa from her cot and placed her in the bath as well. They splashed and played with each other and screamed with delight. I then saw to their dressing and took them downstairs for a breakfast of oatmeal, ham and toast.

After breakfast I set them down in front of the television and put Nickelodeon Jr on which was a bit young for Rosie but she didn't mind letting Melissa have a chance at her favourites then she could have her chance later on. Meanwhile, I continued busying around in the kitchen, when I was satisfied I went back upstairs, hoovered the carpets, changed Melissa's bedding which were also new and dusted her set of little white pieces of furniture. I was just strolling back downstairs when I heard the door bell ring.

I was so excited as I opened the door because I knew it was George and though I saw him only the night before I was already missing him. He was wearing a happy smile when I opened the door and carrying a fresh bunch of red roses. "Merry Christmas Marge." He said happily handing me the flowers. "Merry Christmas to you too and thank you for the beautiful flowers." I responded as I collected them from his hand and stepped aside to let him pass. As he entered the lounge the children jumped out of their seats and Rosie greeted him saying Merry Christmas, while Melissa held onto his left foot and he slowed his pace so she wouldn't fall. He greeted them cheerfully and sat down to watch the television with them.

I was glad that I had made more than enough breakfast because George hadn't had any breakfast and I was more than happy to feed him, especially on Christmas day, so I dished up some breakfast for him and he ate it hungrily. "That was delicious Marge," he said, and I was please with his response. "Thank you," I said as I took his tray back to the kitchen and did a quick tidy up and as everything was well on its way to being cooked I turned the oven on low and went back out to join in the fun and laughter. It wasn't long after that all the board games and electronic games were pulled out and we had a grand time competing against each other. We were starving by 1400 and I proceeded to serve our main meal so everyone took their seat around the table after a quick wash-up and I had placed everything on the table. It was as if everyone was in a mad rush to eat everything in sight and by the time we were all done eating there was hardly anything left that I could salvage for Boxing Day.

"Is it time to open the presents?" Asked Rosie and I replied, "Not just yet Rosie, we have yet to call our relatives and friends." I flipped the television over to BBC News for George to watch and placed the remote control on the coffee table nearby in case he wanted to watch something else. I didn't want to bore him with talks about Christmas to people in Jamaica, America and even England that he hadn't met. I started off by calling my mom. It was 0800 in Jamaica and she had been up now for hours making her preparations for Christmas. She sounded very happy as she answered the phone with a clear crisp voice. I asked her if she had received her gift which I sent for her weeks before and she said "Yes, thank you." I could see the well wrapped box containing the long elegant looking black dress which I bought her laid out under her Christmas tree amongst the countless number of presents she received from everyone else, which consisted of her children, sons and daughter in law, grandchildren, great grandchildren and friends. "I'm just getting the table ready for later." She said and I thought, "Like mother, like daughter." For I myself had set my table hours before we had our Christmas meal. She was having a few relatives and friends over she told me and I knew they would all have a day full of delicious food, that the memory will stick out in their minds for a long time to come.

I called all my siblings in Jamaica next and was glad that they had all received my cards on time, which I usually send every year, within which I placed a small token each. They were all at home preparing for their Christmas meal in one way or another. Each one I talked to, the girls waited eagerly to talk to and I said a quick hello to my nieces and nephews as well. I spoke to my friends in Jamaica as well and it was basically the same routine and because it was practically the same thing we did on Christmas day every year everybody expected my call. Next was England and I spoke to most of my friends, most of whom are still in the Navy, others were out at sea or somewhere on tour overseas where they couldn't be contacted and a few are friends I had before the Navy.

I deliberately left America for later because it was always better to call

April after she and I had opened our gifts so we could gossip about them. We all went back to playing our games and Rosie pleaded with me several times to allow her to open her gifts but I decided to hold out a bit longer. Finally at 1830 I announced that it was time for everyone to open their gifts and Rosie screamed with joy. I took the digital camera from where it stood on the fridge top next to where I stood and took the pictures earlier from time to time as we all ate and set it up now for taking pictures while we open our presents.

We started off with Melissa whom we gave a hand unwrapping her presents to reveal a host of colourful and attractive gifts as she babbled happily. "I was right." I thought as we torn the wrapping off George's gift to her. "He definitely has the qualities of a good father. The large box with Melissa's name written on it so neatly from George was a baby's high chair. He was quick to observe her need for a high chair which I was planning to get her early in the New Year but he had first me to it and was now busy installing it. I was stunned and quickly said thank you to him while Melissa rambled through all her presents trying to decide which one to play with first. Rosie was next in line and she ambitiously went for the biggest present with her name on first which was the one from George. She opened it without delay and was very excited to find out that it was a Wii console. She thanked him happily and quickly moved on to the smaller gifts which she was grateful for but not too excited about. She thanked us all and was itching to go upstairs to set up her Wii console with George's help.

It was my turn next and I was truly excited. I started off with Melissa's gift, which was a sewing kit, which I had bought myself on her behalf. It was bound to come in handy because now that Rosie had been introduced to sewing at school I was missing a few bits from my old sewing kit which is the same one I used when I joined the Navy, for my kit musters. My next gift was a large photo frame from Rosie which I had bought on her behalf. I knew I would have a Christmas photo of us printed and that the frame would be ideal to keep the photo in safe. The third gift was from George and I wondered what it was as I picked up the small box and shook it gently but got no clue. I removed the tasteful wrapping paper with bow and card to complete and opened the box beneath to reveal a navy blue velvet box which I flipped open to reveal an elegant looking Dolce and Gabbana white, leather strap wrist watch with a golden face. I was touched. I thanked George happily and moved on to the next gift he bought me. I began to wonder why he bought two gifts for me instead of one and he must have read it on my face because he quickly supplied that one of the gifts was an early birthday present since my birthday was only three days away. I nodded in understanding and proceeded to open the gift. I unwrapped the neatly done wrapping and found a large bottle of Chanel beneath it. I was astounded. I couldn't believe that he recognized my perfume and then bought me a large one which would save me the trouble of buying any for a while. "This man is quality." I thought, thanking him with a big, bright smile on my face.

Finally it was George's turn to open his gifts and he started by first opening Melissa's gift to him which was a green pen holder and he smiled joyfully as he thanked me for it. Rosie's gift to him was a Parker pen and again he thanked me with a smile. He then thanked Rosie saying it was a brilliant choice but that she shouldn't have and she replied saying it was her mother's choice and that mom just wanted to get something for everyone and I nodded in agreement. Last but not least were my cases which were in a large box which George opened eagerly and seemed pleased with as he thanked me. Rosie was satisfied when all the gifts were open and she wisped George away upstairs to help her set up her Wii console. George picked Melissa up in his hands and they all disappeared upstairs.

I seized the opportunity to call April so that we could have our gossip in peace and quiet. She and her family had just finished their Christmas meal when the phone reverberated in the midst of their loud, cheerful conversations. Straight away she wanted to know what George had got me for Christmas and was right impressed when I told her. I also told her about my early birthday gift and what George got for the girls and she marvelled out loud. She shared with me what she got from Tyrone and her three boys and I was pleased for her. Tyrone had given her a golden necklace while the boys; Norman, Stanley and Jack gave her a sweater, a coat and the youngest, a scarf respectively. She was very pleased with her gifts and with how her day had gone so far. Before long it was time to see the girls off to bed so shortly afterwards I bid her farewell. It was 2200 when I finally tucked the girls into bed and sat down to a drink with George. We were having sorrel which I had brewed weeks before and left to marinade. It was delicious with just a dash of rum. We talked for a while about the day's events when George finally decided it was time he left. He took his coat off the rack and put it on then without warning he swiftly took me in his arms and put my body up against his.

I felt the earth moved as I stood there feeling the powerful force of his body up against mine while I sniffed the special smell intermingled with the sorrel and rum we had just had as he breathed. I wanted him so bad but I couldn't risk it, though I just stood there without putting up any resistance while he looked straight into my eyes. "Marge, I want to thank you for giving me a wonderful Christmas, I have never enjoyed it so much before," he whispered as we continued to make eye contact with the awareness of our bodies touching each other and the hunger we felt for each other. My mind ran on to think of Marvin Gaye's "sexual healing" and before I could think of something to say he kissed my forehead and was out the door.

MOVING FORWARD

I was wearing an imitation black puffed sleeves couture dress which I had bought recently on the high street which was quality without the high price. I felt I had exhausted two of my original couture dresses and was saving the third in case a very special occasion arose. I quickly applied my sheer cover and checked my black shiny perm hair again which was very neatly combed without a strand out of place and was resting just below my shoulders. "George will be here soon." I thought, as I stood and checked myself out in the mirror. My knee length high boots made me look tall and elegant and with them combined with everything else I looked no less than stunning. I sprayed my Chanel behind my ears and grabbed my black hand bag just in time to hear the door bell ring.

I hurried downstairs, opened the front door and there he was, the man of my dreams. He looked well put together as usual in a blue short sleeve shirt and a smooth white jeans which you had no way of knowing was jeans until you felt the material. His track shoes were black and sleek and looked like a modern pair of Clark's. He looked more handsome than ever before and I took one look at him and squirmed inside with excitement and immediately had to fight to hold it together. "Hi. You alright?" He asked and I quickly replied, "Yes." And stepped aside. "Would you like to come in for a bit?" I asked and he said, "No thanks, it's alright." Which is what I was hoping he would say. It wasn't very often that he would come to mine and it just made me nervous because I was so worried that he might see something out of place and think that I wasn't a good home maker. "Shall we go then?" I said and we walked together at an even pace to the car.

George quickly got to my side of the car and opened the door for me and then he jumped in behind the steering wheel. He drove at a steady and even pace as we talked about the girls and laughed and sighed more than we exchanged words as we did and it was clear to me how much he was fund of them. I felt so lucky. Not only was he charming sweet, hot and handsome but he also cares immensely for me and the girls. The day was bright and sunny and I felt like heaven was shining its light of wellness and goodwill down upon me. When we finally got to Trafford Centre George took my hand and told me to close my eyes and I did easily because George had said a few days ago when he asked me out on a date with him today that it was a surprise date. I had no idea what he meant but I trusted him with every breath that I breathe. He took my hand in his as he lead me slowly and firmly while walking by my side. I could feel that he had turned off into a shop but I had no idea what shop it was. It felt like I was touching a showcase when he said in a quiet voice, "Marge, open your eyes now."

I opened my eyes and realized that we were standing in the centre of a jewellery store and everyone in the store was looking at me now, I felt embarrassed. I was just standing there looking at him not knowing the meaning of it all until he pointed at the show case and said, "Is there anything in here that you like?" I was tongue tied as I looked closely at where he was pointing and it hit me that they were all engagement rings, beautiful, fanciful engagement rings. I glanced at some of the prices above the skilfully designed rings, neatly arranged in rows both vertically and horizontally. I wondered for a bit if he was joking and looked at his face to find a smirk but instead found his usual sincere and caring countenance as he waited for me patiently. I looked back at the show case and thought hard about the ring I might like to wear as a bond between George and myself to represent the love and respect I feel so deeply for him. I saw a glam looking ring which was made of yellow gold with diamonds on either side and a diamond shaped elevated top with diamond stones encrusted all over it. "It looks very expensive," I thought and quickly compared the price to all the other rings in the show case. "Blimey!" I thought, "it's the most expensive ring in the show case by far."

At the same time a sales representative walked over to us and asked, "Can I help?" George looked at me and asked, "Have you chosen anything yet?" and I find myself blush because the only one I liked and had spent time contemplating was the most expensive one. I looked up at George, quickly composed myself and pointed to the ring. "That one," I said. "I see you have an expensive taste," he smiled and without delay asked the sales representative to please allow us to have a close look at it. I was too stunned to respond to his musing and just stood there and watched while everything seemed to happen in slow motion. The sales rep gave him the ring and he took it confidently and purposefully and offered it to me in his open palm. I looked down at it in his palm and it dazzled even more up close. It was gorgeous. I took it calmly and put it on my ring finger conscious of being watched by him, the sales rep and others in the store who were watching us from we entered the store, I can imagine, as my eyes were shut. I just stood there looking at it and glanced up only to see George gazing through his big pretty eyes at me with such tenderness and I swear I felt his love hitting me like a bolt. "Do you like it?" He asked like he already knew the answer and I nodded and he responded, "I like it too Marge and I think it suits you very well."

I was overjoyed and had a hard time keeping my composure. I was surprised at how well the ring fit when I tried to take it back off and had to use some force. I finally got it off and put it back in George's open palm and he handed it to the sales rep who asked if we were happy and put the ring in a box. Afterwards we just strolled quietly, arm in arm along the shops in the centre and finally stopped for something to eat in a cosy Chinese restaurant in China Town, Trafford Centre. We ate a three course meal and slowly strolled to the cinema where we watched the film 'Big Mama, like father like son" which was full of fun and excitement. We had a great time and when George dropped me back home and the baby sitter left, the girls were all over him vying for his attention as I made him a cup of tea. Rosie wanted him to play games with her on her Wii console and Melissa just wanted him to lift her up and talk baby talk to her because whenever he stopped talking baby talk to her and put her down she would get a bit fussy. In the end I had to take Melissa who was due her feed anyway and announced that it was time to play on the Wii console. It was very late when they finished and because it was the weekend and she hardly ever played on the Wii console I wasn't bothered by it.

It was about 2345 when George gave me a hand getting them off to bed and it puzzled me that I hadn't seen them so happy in a long time. Normally they would be fussing with each other while competing for my attention. I knew he was the perfect father for them and also the perfect husband for me. "Why don't you stay here tonight?" I asked as I shifted the lounge curtain and saw the rain pounding down on the window pane. It was jet black and based on the amount of heat it was taking to warm the house I could tell that the temperature had dropped dramatically. He glanced at his wrist watch and looked at me gently. "Are you sure Marge? Because I really don't mind the rain you know and it's never too wet or cold for me." "Don't be silly George," I said. "I'll bring some blankets down for you." I crawled into bed just after mid night and felt happy beyond belief. I couldn't believe that my life had turned around so unrecognizably in such a short space of time. I went off to sleep in a state of bliss.

I was awoken by the flushing of the toilet and looked at the clock on my bedside table, it was 0230. I wanted to check that everything was alright so I threw my dressing gown and bed slippers on and quickly mounted the landing, only to see that it was George who had used the toilet and was swiftly making his way back down to the sofa where I had left him to get his head down just after midnight. He slowed in his steps when he saw me and smiled relaxingly. "Are you alright, Marge?" He asked smiling and I felt like a fool for putting myself into this position. I was enthralled by him and so it took me a while to realize that I was just stood there staring at him and by that time it was too late for me to do anything because he had got to where I was standing and was holding my hands in his and looking down at me. "I'm alright." I heard myself say and even I was not convinced by it.

He was still looking down at me and smiling minutes after and all that was going through my head was how much I wanted to be with him. I also knew I had to control myself especially now that the children were around. He must have read my thoughts because he slowly placed his lips on mine and held me in his powerful embrace as he caressed my lips with his. I thought I had died and gone to heaven because I couldn't believe how much of a good kisser he was on top of everything else that was perfect about him. He led me gently to the open door with the dim light of my bedside lamp pouring out and I followed obediently. He closed my bedroom door and slowly took my dressing gown off. I was exploding inside.

He then led me into bed and lay himself down next to me then pulled the cover over our bodies. I thought I was having a blissful dream. I thought of pinching myself but decided against it because I felt so good and I preferred to believe it was real even if it was a dream. I was wearing a skimpy, black negligee. As I lay there wondering what would happen next I felt him reach for me effortlessly with his long hands across to my side of the bed and I completely lost it. I had that feeling of locked lust as he took my body commandingly and held it close to his; he again placed his lips more forcefully this time on top of mine and stroked them passionately. I was out of breath and even felt my body shiver in his arms. "Don't worry sweet Marge," He said, "I will never hurt you." As he said that in an ever so soft, sincere and tender voice I felt emotions rushed through me and I could also feel wetness between my legs.

He then rested my head on his chest and the feel of it drove me wild. "Goodnight Marge." I heard him say and I thought to myself that he must be an angel out of heaven because he never seeks to take advantage of me during my moments of extreme weakness. I just lie there thinking about how much I wish I could just ravish him but when I thought about how he might think of me after that I just let the thought go. I realized I couldn't take any chances because I could never lose him as he had come to mean so much to me. A few minutes after that I could hear him snoring quietly. It was at least half hour afterwards that I fell asleep in his arms and when he held me tight and kissed me once more in the first light of morning I wondered how I survived the night. He kissed me again and again. I was so excited I thought my wetness would soil the bed and he would notice. I felt a bit ashamed but couldn't respond to this feeling because I was so overwhelmed with love and desire for him.

He let me go and climbed off the bed onto his knees. "Marge," he said, holding the box that he got the day before from the jewellers in one hand, "You are beautiful, very courageous, strong, intelligent and amazingly sweet and kind. You have come into my life and changed it forever. I love you so much and our girls. This is why I am asking you now Marge, will you marry me?" I looked up into his eyes and he was so sincere I thought he might cry, his eyes were moist and it was just so emotional and articulate, the way he proposed. I felt like I was going to break down and cry because of how perfectly beautiful everything was. I didn't want to spoil everything so I bit on my lip to stay focussed. "I will." I said and he confidently put the delicate diamond ring on my finger. He then examined my hand closely and kissed it softly.

He came back into bed beside me and held me gently in his arms while he held my head back and kissed my lips hungrily, deeper this time and more impatiently and I knew I had been ready for a while, and he as well. He moved his other hand gently along the back of my silky negligee and caressed my firm buttocks, then used both hands to squeeze either side of my buttocks. I was getting wetter and wetter and my body trembled in agony. With his lips still on mine he ran his hand across my bosom and took his second hand from between my buttocks where he was moving his finger back and forth gently. He placed both hands on my bosom and squeezed it and removed his lips from mine to place them at the top of my bosom as he gently kissed and slowly licked them and simultaneously squeezed my breasts together which were bulging with need, I could feel that my nipples had become tender and swollen.

He slowly took the top of my negligee off and now my breasts were exposed. I purred in ecstasy as he took my nipples in his mouth and sucked them gently as he held onto my bottom with his big wide strong hands. I wanted to weep in elation, to throw my rear end in the air and do the dutty wine, to scream pussy cloth at the top of my lungs or to just jump on top of him and just let it all go but I couldn't bring myself to do any of them. Instead I just lay there marvelling at the feelings that were radiating through me. He then felt between my legs which was as wet as a river and he sighed in disbelief and quickly shifted his position, his nose now sniffing at my wetness I was sure I screamed but was too caught up in the moment to even realize it.

He swiftly removed my g-string in one swift movement and hungrily but gently ate, sucked and licked at my wetness. I was completely swamped with ecstasy and vaguely remember screaming his name passionately. By the time he mounted me with his firm well proportioned joy stick I was more than up for it. Before I knew it I was moving rhythmically to his thrusts, clawing at his back and screaming his name. His thrusts got faster and faster as he moved in and out powerfully with the agility of a lion. We moved together for a while and I needed him so badly I was afraid I would never get enough of him. His last thrusts were the most powerful yet as he groaned, "Oh Marge, oh Marge." And held my hips firm to restrict my movements while at the same time thrusting deeper and deeper inside me. Tears were streaming down my face by then, I realized I was still shivering in ecstasy and no sooner I could feel myself exploding inside like a burst hydrant. He gave one last quick, powerful, deep thrust with a loud groan and then lay on top of me shivering and breathing heavily.

We were there like that in silence for a while then he slowly moved down again to my wetness and licked and sucked it until it was dry. As he lay beside me again he held my face up to his and as he gently looked into my eyes he said, "Marge, I didn't hurt you did I?" He kissed the tears from my face as I said softly, "I love you." And he kissed my lips gently for a while and then replied. "I love you too sweetheart. We need to set a date for our wedding."

It was still early and I was relieved that the girls were still fast asleep when George showered and left. I had offered him breakfast and he told me not to trouble myself but to just stay in bed and get some more rest. He then hugged me and gave me a soft gentle kiss on my lips and I could smell the freshness of his breath and taste the sweetness of his saliva. I just wanted to carry on kissing him and doing things to him and never let him go. "Marge," He said as he stood up, looking straight into my eyes, "I love you and will always take care of you and the girls." "I love you too." I said. "Marge," he said again in a calm voice, "would you please call your mom for me." I was a bit puzzled by his request but I was so pleased and happy with him that he could never ask too much. "Yes, I will sweetheart." I said and he said good bye quietly and left. I wondered when he left why it was so important for me to call mom. Of course he had spoken to her on several occasions by now and I could tell that they liked each other and were building a good relationship but what was happening in Jamaica that I didn't already know about. I pushed the thought of my mom out of my mind and reflected on my first sexual contact with George. Oh my God, I just couldn't relive it enough. I was totally blissed up. "I couldn't be any happier," I thought. I must have fallen asleep, thinking about him because I woke up to the sound of Melissa's chattering.

I switched off the monitor and looked at the clock, it was 0836. About 1100 I decided to call my mom, I put in the international code, the country code and then the local telephone number and listened while the phone rang. I was hoping that nothing bad had happened to my family and friends back in Jamaica. I physically crossed my fingers and prayed silently. The girls were in the lounge watching Rasta Mouse on CBBC. I had seen to the girls' bath, fed them a healthy breakfast of cereal, eggs and toast and set them down in front of the television so that I could focus on my conversation with my mom without any noise or interruptions. I was still overjoyed with my engagement and being with George and was now closely scrutinizing the precious ring on my finger.

It seemed so familiar and felt so right. "Hello," I heard in the phone, it was my mom on the other end of the line sounding her usual proper and together self even at 0500 Jamaica time. I preferred to ring her early so that my call wouldn't interfere with anything she might have planned for the day. She is usually up quite early anyway. "Oh hi mom," I said and she sounded so happy and pleased to hear me that I knew straight away that everything was alright in Jamaica, I could now relax and think about my good news which I couldn't wait to share with my mom.

I find that I was always more than happy to share good news with my family and particularly my mom but I was never please or even too willing to share bad news with them. Two of my sisters, April and Althea are the ones who usually have to contend with the bad news, especially April and also one of my good and close friends Kelly. Tiffany, Lucy, Samantha and my other friends in the Navy, at one point or other, were a part of my support system when I've had to deal with bad news but at times when I needed them they were away at sea, unreachable so, though no fault of their own, they were not always reliable.

"Is everything alright dear," she said. "I'm fine mom." I said and for a split second felt so home sick I thought I was going to cry. I cleared my throat and asked if she was alright and she said, "How is that young man of yours, has he proposed yet?" I was shocked because I had not mentioned anything about my engagement to her. George and I though we were very happy together and only God knows who didn't know about our happiness because I introduced him to all my family, friends and anyone who cared to know, over the phone because everyone was either overseas, living miles away in the south of England, or a few in Birmingham.

Only a handful of people who cared to know were living in Manchester and they knew all about him from earlier on. "Wah?" I said, unable to contain my surprise. "Don't worry dear," my mom said, still calm. "I'm not psychic or anything." And that came as a bit of news to me because while I was growing up I was sure that my mom was a bit psychic because she always knew when we did anything wrong. "George called me three days ago and asked me for your hand in marriage." I was gobsmacked. I had no idea. I felt proud that my man, of all the men I've known, took the initiative to ask my mom for my hand in marriage. I couldn't believe it. Tears welled up in my eyes as I thought about how absolutely wonderful he is and how for the short time I had known him, though it felt like we had known each other for many years that no one I have ever known could possibly fill his shoes. I thought about my father at this point and of the great man he was. I was forced to think that George might be out doing even my father. I was truly amazed.

My mom got concerned when a few seconds passed and she didn't hear me. "Dear," she said, "are you still there?" "Yes, I'm still here mom," I said and she continued. "How could I say no to such a gentleman?" "I could tell that both of you were right for each other from the start." She said and I thought to myself that she really must like him because she usually doesn't think much of most of the other men in my life. I started thinking of the many times I defied my mom and went against her advice and thought of how much grief I would have saved myself if only I had listened. "You do know of course that you have to give me enough time to plan your wedding and get it right." She said and right away I knew that our wedding would have to be held in Jamaica.

THE STYLE FAMILY

It was a long flight home to Jamaica and we had got up, prepared ourselves and left out very early in order to check in our luggage early and be there on time for our flight. As usual Manchester airport was packed with people both arriving and departing the airport. We were tired now and were already feeling jet logged as the day's events were taking their toll on us. George was holding Melissa who had already slept several times throughout our journey and was getting a bit fussy now. I gave George another bottle of feed for her that I had just taken from the glove compartment.

I turned back to continue my conversation with Rosie who herself had slept laying back in her seat with her feet up for a while and was now so tired of staying in one place that she was making regular visits up and down the passage to the toilet just so that she could stretch her legs. I felt a bit guilty for putting the girls through it all but I also felt comforted by the thought that they would be able to get a long quiet break at my mom's, where I grew up, which was comfortable and peaceful. I felt a bit dreary and wondered quietly for a minute. I was used to travelling at unsociable hours, what with having being a student and having served in the Navy. I pushed it out of my mind and turned back to Rosie. "So, what is sixteen plus nineteen plus twenty seven?" each time I would try to give her a problem that she might not be able to work out in her head to challenge her but she always came back with the correct answer. She was a figure head, a maths whizz. I was proud of her and always encouraged her to do more.

Melissa sucked noisily at the bottle with dreamy eyes as George fed her and as soon as she sucked all the feed from the bottle she fell into a deep sleep, curled up in his arms. George held her proudly in his arms and smiled. It was amazing how good he was with Melissa. She never had any problems falling asleep in his arms. It would be always after a feed and whenever he would rock her softly and gently in his arms. She never seemed to fuss when she was with him. She expected a good time playing with him and he always delivered. She would often seek his attention by holding onto his foot while he walked in the lounge, putting her face up to his and smiling her mischievous smile or by repeating whatever he said and he never ignored her no matter what he was doing.

I was listening to a very nostalgic station with my ear plugs and I wanted to share it with him so I took the one on his side and offered it to him and he smile knowingly at me while he listened to the rich, smooth lyrics of Dennis Brown. Not long afterwards Rosie returned from one of her trips to the toilet and curled up in her seat with her head on my shoulder. Soon after she was snoring softly and George put Melissa in her car seat that was on the seat next to him, which was padded with blankets and covered her over, she looked just like an angel as she slept soundly.

George then reached for me, wrapped his hands around the nape of my head and kissed me repeatedly, I felt like I was flying with my own wings, then he stared into my eyes with his face close to mine and used his thumbs to slowly rub my cheeks. I felt the hair stand up all over my body, and then he put his lips up to my ear, kissed it softly and whispered, "Oh Marge, I love you so much." I wanted to cry and I whispered in response, "I love you so much too sweetheart." He kept staring into my eyes for another while and then he released my head, sat back in his chair and took my hand in his. He kissed it several times as he rubbed it and massaged it in between then eventually he leaned his shoulder towards me and carefully put my head down to rest on his shoulder. I didn't realize how tired I was but before long I was fast asleep.

I remember thinking about my wedding dress which I bought myself because though my mom was true to her word as she always was anyway and planned our wedding for us I didn't want to take any chances with the dress because I felt I had to put it on in order to be satisfied that it really covered the contours of my body extremely well. I wanted to be able to show off my family and myself this time because too often memories of my first wedding would come back to me like a plague of how plain my first wedding was because Roger and I had planned to wed in Cornwall, England but when I went to Jamaica on Easter holiday we wed then instead of waiting and doing it properly and so everything was quite rushed. I was puzzled at how I still felt a bit embarrassed to let anyone see our wedding pictures and the fact that there was no DVD recording of the event. After Roger and I got married and he joined me in Cornwall I would always ask him to let us have a proper wedding one day so we could get decent pictures of me in a proper wedding dress and he always said it wasn't necessary.

I was so happy that I was so in love with George and that I didn't have to do what a lot of people do when they think they are at that point in their lives when they can't afford to fall in love anymore but just have to be content with having a partner. I felt like everything was like a lesson to me, a learning curve preparing me for my relationship with George. Knowing that he was so happy with the girls was a confirmation of my beliefs. George also had his tanned suit which was well tailored and was the only thing which was in the suitcase with my dress apart from the girls' mini-bride dresses. I was real careful not to put anything else with them that might crush or soil them. They were very expensive garments which we'll only be wearing once but I felt as though it was absolutely worth it and that the moment we got dressed on our wedding day which was only two days away we would be getting our money's worth.

I was also hoping that Rosie will be more than happy on that special day when she wed many years from now, to wear my dress with pride. I was awoken by the pilot's voice telling us that we would shortly be arriving in Jamaica. I knew that because the flight was all of eight and a half hours when the pilot made his announcement we usually have about an hour and a half left to go. I checked around and saw that the girls were still sleeping and George was wide awake as usual. I could tell he was in deep thoughts and he also looked a bit nervous about meeting my family for the first time.

In an attempt to calm him down and relax him I told him of how the United Kingdom always had very close ties to Jamaica. I talked about Bob Marley, the true legend of Reggae music and how his father was English and his mother Jamaican, of Winston Churchill and how much he was glorified and revered in Jamaica and of the astoundingly beautiful and very generous and down to earth Princess Dianna and how much the announcement of her death left a large hole in the pit of our stomachs that would never be filled again. I was a very young girl when I first heard about Bob Marley. I had gone to visit my father at the UWI's Students Union where he was a Chef. He had started off at the Student Union doing odd jobs when he was only nine years old as he had run away from his family in St. Elizabeth when he felt he wasn't being treated equally or as well as his step siblings.

My father's story which I always marvelled at has always been one of survival, wisdom and strength to me. He was later employed as a Handy Man and afterwards as a Caretaker of the Student Union, living in a house just to the back of the Student Union with his family. Well, I was sitting down waiting for my father and my eyes caught a group of students, mostly males, in the bar of the Students Union who were talking about the music as they fiercely compared Jacob miller to Bob Marley, there were at least two Rastafarians among them who were largely the ones who saw the true value of the Music in those days.

Some of them were of the belief that Jacob Miller was a better performer than Bob Marley, that it was because of Bob Marley's background why he was getting the recognition he did back then, and of course others within the group argued bitterly that Bob Marley was truly talented which is why he was being lorded both nationally and internationally. I had never seen Bob Marley perform nor hear his music at that point in my life because my mother was never having it but one thing I was sure of was of the powerful effect of the Music to a few, especially the Rastafarians.

It was my aunt from August Town and her family, who I remember talking about Sir Winston Churchill with great respect and admiration. She had and probably still has a large picture in a golden frame of him in her front room to this day. Though there was a lot of controversy in Jamaica surrounding his rule and the decisions he made during the Second World War I know that most Jamaicans respect the stance he took against Germany and the Hitler regime.

Finally, Princess Dianna, I remember how I used to read constantly of her journeys across the globe, helping and supporting the sick, the starved and the destitute. It just seemed like she devoted all of her life to giving of herself. I was always touched by her and how she treated people who were not as fortunate as herself and especially because she didn't have to. She could have done a few visits I suppose and everyone would have been satisfied but she was so generous, she gave of her heart. People in her position can be vain, wicked and self centred but never Princess Dianna. It was midnight when I had gone to bed early which was against the norm for me because from I was very young I would stay up until very late every night as if I was afraid of missing something while I slept.

I remember one night as I scurried around the house after midnight trying to figure out what each of the pieces of instruments was for in my older sister's mathematical set, my mother got upset with me and complained to my father and I can still hear his voice as he told her, "Don't worry, let her stay up for a bit longer, she is going to be a bright girl." I was a bit surprised at his answer to my mom but ever since that night I found that I always tried to live up to my father's expectations of me.

Anyway, my sister Vicky called me on my mobile on 31st of august 1997 and told me that there was breaking news of Princess Dianna who was involved in an accident and that I should switch on the news. Though I was sleepy I instantly jumped out of bed and switched on the television. The news which ran for hours on end right back into morning and for most of the next day spoke of how Princess Dianna was feared dead at first as she was involved in a car crash and later that she had died as a result of the car crash which was caused by paparazzi. For the next couple of days, weeks and even months most of the media spent most if not all of their time on news of Dianna's life and her subsequent death. It was like a gloom had covered the skies of Jamaica. No one could avoid empathizing with the Princess and following her story. Some people in Jamaica still can't believe that Princess Dianna could have died in the way she did. It is odd.

As the plain descended we saw the last of the sunshine which lay over the beautiful landscapes of St. Andrew. The plane landed and we collected our suitcases and eagerly went through customs. It was just starting to get dark when we collected the keys for the large transit van which we had arranged for the rental of before hand from the rent a car company at the airport. As we pulled out of Norman Manley airport, named after one of Jamaica's former prime ministers, and drove through the streets of Kingston it was dark and signs of the Jamaican night life was coming to as in various hot spots we could see crowds gathering to begin their evening's celebrations.

We arrived at Payton Place only about thirty minutes after and all eagerly piled into the cosy, homely living room where I grew up. I glanced around excitedly and saw my mom approaching me with open arms, the lot of my siblings, except for April who was based overseas, were seated all about the room and they all approached us with words of greetings and welcomed George to the family. I hugged and kissed my mom and for a moment I thought she wasn't going to let me go and then she finally released me and moved on to greet George and welcome him to the family. She finally took over the girls, Melissa up in her arms and held onto Rosie's hand as she led them off into the kitchen asking, "What would you like to eat girls?"

George sat next to me and I held his hand in support as I knew what was coming next, the famous family grilling which was like an interview, but only a bit less stressful and more fun, by all in the family each time a new person joined the Style family. He was grilled by my five sisters and two brothers who were present. Whenever I felt they were going overboard I would quickly butt in so that George wouldn't have to deal with it. A while afterwards my mom came back and told us that the girls were sleeping and that she would talk to us tomorrow after we had a good night's rest. She then announced that our evening meal was ready and we all gathered into the dining room around the large table.

We all ate and enjoyed our mom's cooking, as usual, which was rice and peas and ox-tail for the main course and even George complimented her on how delicious the food tasted and she proudly thanked him. George was not quite used to Jamaican dishes yet though I had fed him rice and peas on several occasions but he was really developing an appreciation for all things Jamaican. Mom excused herself and said she was a bit tired and was taking an early night. She quickly walked us through my old room and explained that she had just put on clean bedding, a couple of towels and toiletries were placed in the closet and chest of drawers which were for our use. The girls were in the room right next door to ours and we quickly took the opportunity to check on them and kiss them good night.

After that we went back to the living room where everyone was awaiting us to continue with their grilling. It was way past midnight when we all seemed to decide at the same time that we would make it a night. I knew that if I wanted to have some peace and quiet with George in Jamaica before our wedding day we would have to make our get away in a few hours before anyone was up. We said our good nights and tiredly strolled off to bed. As soon as we got into bed George held me close to him and kissed me several times and we fell asleep almost instantaneously in each other's arms.

It was the need to urinate that woke me up and as I opened my eyes lazily and looked at the clock I realized it was 0530, just a few hours after we got our head down, but I knew how crucial it was to postpone the sleep and get a head start to somewhere safe before we were caught up in the web of my family again who thought it was their responsibility since our father had passed away to keep up the grilling tradition.

It was good to know that the family was supportive and was looking out for your best interest but at times it could get in the way of good ordinary fun and enjoyment. I quickly urinated and had a quick shower which took me about five minutes in my haste. I went back into the room and looked at George sleeping deeply and I felt so guilty for waking him because he looked so tired. I thought about letting him sleep but I knew it would be even worse on our wedding day if we didn't take some time out for a break now. I shook him steadily while whispering his name and he jumped out of his sleep and looked up at me. I then reminded him that we had to get a move on from early so he had his shower which was not quite as short as mine but it gave me a chance to make myself pretty. I chose a cute little floral top and a pair of jeans shorts, happy that I could dress skimpily because the weather was warm and mostly sunny.

I carefully applied my make up, aware that if I didn't wear enough it would disappear within minutes of leaving the house because of the warmth and put on my Timberland loafers. George was out of the shower now and dressing when I quickly scribbled a note for the girls, telling we had to leave out early but would see them later and left it on their bed side table. I then wrote my mom a note telling her that we would be back just after mid day because I knew she would be up early fussing about breakfast for us and wanting to reconfirm all the wedding arrangements with us. A part of me wanted to take the girls with us but I know that my mom would take good care of them until we got back which would be better than trying to care for them in the van. Also, they would make too much noise and would alert everyone before we made our get away. George put on his knee length jeans and a close fitting Nike t- shirt.

We carefully snuck into the van and quietly drove away and as soon as we were safely away we giggled and cheered at our genius. There was so much I wanted to show him but for today I had to settle for places in our close vicinity. First there was the UWI Chapel gardens, then Sovereign Centre and finally Devon House, a great house where we could park the van and have a snooze before heading back home. We decided to go to the nearest and the one which was also closest to my heart first so we pulled into the UWI main gate and I proudly told George, "This is my alma marter." We headed straight for the University Chapel and parked at the bottom of the long path which divided the garden into two that overlooked the main gate and the Pure and Applied Sciences faculty.

It was still a bit dark when we got there as day was only just beginning to break and George pulled me into his arms and kissed me hungrily and I kissed him in return only just realizing how much I was hungry for his touch. We were in the back of the van when he stroked my hair and opened the front of my blouse to kiss my swollen breasts. I had a flash of memories of times I spent with Chris in the garden when I was at my peak. I wondered why it was felt that people had more sexual desire at a certain age of life because looking back now, it is the same intensity I feel with George as I felt with Chris.

In fact, if I may be blunt I was feeling even more intensity and emotions with George than at any other time in my life. My body was full of need for him and I wasn't prepared to wait too long, neither was he I gathered. He was feeling my wetness now and I held onto his joy stick in response. He quickly tasted my juice and I screamed with delight and hurriedly took his joystick and placed it inside me because I just felt so horny and full of lust. He seemed happy with my action and groaned eagerly while we moved together rhythmically. I shouted his name in ecstasy and he responded each time by thrusting even deeper and harder and time seemed to disappear as we got lost in each others tight embrace. We were totally nockered when George groaned his final load throaty groan and thrust so deep and hard in me I wanted to cry but saved by the fact that it was ever so sweet. We continued to hold each other tight and close when it was all over and drifted off to sleep in each others arms.

We woke up to the sound of students and staff of the campus busying about and we hurriedly cleaned up ourselves and put our clothes back on. We left the van and strolled around the garden admiring its quiet beauty and watching the many students who were sitting all about the garden, preparing papers for presentations, studying for exams or just reading their text books. It took us a while before we realize how hungry we were and we slowly strolled back to the van. We had to get some breakfast before it was too late and I decided that a Campus breakfast would be ideal. It was a while since I had a Campus breakfast, several years ago in fact, before I left Jamaica to join the RN. I liked the meals on Campus; they were always tastily prepared in the true tradition of Jamaican cuisine.

I directed George a few minutes later to Taylor Hall for breakfast. Taylor Hall is where I had most of my Campus meals even though Mary Seacole Hall (The female only hall) is the hall I should have been committed to. Except that there was something about the food at Taylor Hall, it just seemed to be somewhat sweeter than the food from any other hall, though I have had occasion to enjoy food from other halls of the Campus. It was as if I was trying to make up for all the years without most of the Jamaican dishes that I grew up eating when I ordered ackee and salt fish with fried dumplings, callaloo and boiled bananas and roast yam, a bowl of corn meal porridge and two cups of chocolate tea. George and I then drove back to the chapel gardens and we both dived in and ate to our hearts content. When we were finished we took a general drive around the Campus where

I showed him the different places of interest to me then we headed off to the Sovereign Centre in Liguanea.

We walked about the different stores and marvelled at the items on sale and when we had had enough we finally took off to Devon House where we bought ice cream and walked the full length of the property, hand in hand talking about my previous trips to Devon House and the surrounding areas. Jet log took its toll and we went back to the van which was parked in the quiet among the trees and slept for a while, holding onto each other. It was nearly noon when we woke up and we were ready for a solid lunch so headed back along hope road to Liguanea and grabbed some tastee patties from Sugar and Spice Bakery which were just as delicious as I remember. We washed them down with orange juice and went on our way home to face the music.

As we approached the living room we were aware of the presence of my siblings because of their loud roars of laughter as they joked around with each other. I thought to myself, "If this lot is as loud as this, what will be the result when their spouses and children, April and her family, and other relatives and friends joined in on our wedding day, which was the following day; and especially at the reception later in the evening?" Nervousness was starting to creep in and when I looked at George's face I felt he was thinking the same thing. "He is going to get cold feet and back out!" I thought worriedly. My mom cut in, in front of everyone, held onto our hands and led us straight into the dining room where she made us tea and bought us time by having a very relaxed conversation with us and generally making pleasantries. The girls were taken to the zoo at Hope Gardens and would afterwards be taken to the cinema at sovereign Centre for a kiddies' movie by Catherine, a family friend, so we could have some time to ourselves my mom informed us. She then went over the details of the wedding and reminded us that our wedding rehearsal was later on in the evening. When she finally handed us back to my siblings we only had to bear about an hour of grilling before all of us had to prepare ourselves and head for the church. We all sat around the dining table where we were fed yet another delicious meal then we headed off to the church. My siblings left just ahead of us as most of them were collected one by one by their spouse. My mom was the first to leave as she had to see to the order and organization of everything.

George and I left out after everyone had gone because we wanted to build up our nerves a bit; after all, this was our wedding we were about to rehearse. He held me in his arms and kissed me deeply and tenderly several times. "Marge, I love you, but are you sure this is what you want?" He asked looking deep into my soul and I felt a bit scared and surprised by the question, like a child about to be abandoned by her parents but I decided to just dismiss it as in my mind the time for uncertainties had passed a long time ago, not that I ever had any. I was fully aware though that it was a whole different story in a man's world. "Are you kidding me? You bet!" I said firmly in an effort to eliminate all his doubts. I then continued in a very soft voice, "you know I love you sweetheart, more than I have ever loved anyone else and I know you love me very much too so there." He nodded his head in agreement but still had a confused look upon his face. "We should go," he said checking himself in the mirror.

He looked as handsome and sexy as usual in his Bench jeans and navy blue t-shirt which clung to him and showed his musclilly chest. As I stood beside him in the mirror I became aware of how tall he was and fetching, very very fetching. I looked at myself and was pleased, my pink floral dress which was a bit above my knees was very tasty and brought out the radiance in my appearance and my hair which was falling about the top of my back and about my face looked shinier than ever. I stepped into a brown pair of pumps which goes well with my dress, grabbed my brown handbag and re-did my orange lipstick. "Yeah, you are right, we should go." I said and we walked together to the van and drove to the church. Everyone was already there when we arrived back at the University chapel, except for the girls and my nephew Cal but they wouldn't be attending the rehearsal as they would just be showed briefly what they needed to do in the morning prior to the wedding. It wasn't rocket science anyway. There was a happy vibe in the air and though they had taken their positions they were standing real easy talking and laughing with each other.

We went right in and my mom got us into position and announced that we would now begin. We went through the routine a few times from start to finish and it all ran smoothly, what worried me though was the look on George's face. It was the same look he had when he asked me if I was sure I wanted to go through with our wedding and it never changed. Each time he was asked to say his vows the look came back and lasted until he was told to kiss the bride. I was seriously worried now and I knew that I couldn't talk to anyone about it because if I did everyone would know about it by the morning and by then my life would be a disaster. We greeted everyone we were seeing for the first time since we got to Jamaica and I introduced George around quickly and left along with everyone else.

I reached for one of the CD's randomly on the dash board and put it in the CD player as soon as we sat in the van to lighten our mood. Without warning Yellow Man's "I'm getting married in the morning" rang out in our ears and George switched it off right away with the same look from before upon his face as he avoided my eyes. We were quiet all the way home and as soon as we returned he told me that my brother had made arrangements for him to stay over at theirs' after a few drinks and a night out clubbing with all the adult males in the family and their close friends at one of Kingston's hot spots and then he would leave from there straight to the church in the morning. At first I felt a bit resentful at the thought that I wasn't told about the plans they had made for George for the night earlier but then I decided it might be the thing to cheer him up and bring him back to his senses so I agreed with a smile.

I was just about to prepare for bed when I heard a knock at the door. I thought that George had forgotten something and had returned to pick it up. "What have you forgotten?" I said opening the door. "Hey, get ready; we are going to hit the town!" My sister Amanda announced as she barged into the room past me. My mouth was still gaping wide open when the other five, including my sister in law, Beth, came in behind her. They were all dressed up in the latest clubbing gear. "Did you think we were going to let you get away?" Said Althea and Vicky joined in and said "You thought we were going to leave you by yourself tonight so you could drive yourself crazy just thinking about your big day tomorrow?" They all laughed in a chorus and cheered at the thought that they managed to surprise me successfully.

They were so right and I was happy they had come to rescue me from my loneliness and my worries of George. "Thank you guys for saving me." I wanted to say, but pride got in the way and the words stuck in my throat so that all I did was smile a cheeky smile and frowned while protesting. "You could have at least told me so that I would have enough time to prepare myself and I could have told George where I would be, what if he wanted to reach me?" I pleaded." "He's not supposed to speak to you, now until he sees you at the altar." They said in a chorus and I realized how right they were about this too. Because my previous wedding was at such short notice I wasn't allowed the opportunity to follow traditions but at least this time around I was able to do things right and hopefully get it right as well. Before I could get the thought out I found I was thinking about George's reaction to the marriage lately again and I just couldn't bear it anymore so I hurriedly pulled on a pair of close fitting trousers which was thin and hugged my body perfectly, a silk blouse with a zip in the front instead of buttons and a pair of ankle length boots.

I freshened up my make up and before long we were in Quad night club moving between the different clubs inside it which were all on different levels but all under one roof. There was a selection of Dancehall, R&B, Oldies, Dance music and a very current fast paced music with which I was not very familiar. I was puzzled at the speed at which our music changes. We moved from club to club, always forming a circle so that we could talk to and share with each other. We danced up a storm with them always trying to show me the latest dance moves to almost every song as it came on. Each dance move has its own name and I caught on to many of the dance moves which I was so excited to learn and take back with me but there were a few that were just too much for me to catch onto in one night. There were songs that I hadn't heard in ages like Bob Marley's "I don't wanna wait in vain for your love", "I wanna love you" and so many more, especially in the oldies club, which made me think of George and I had to just push thoughts of him out of my mind and revelled in the goodness of the music.

There were times when we were just too tired to dance and we just stood around talking and giggling like when we were in high school which made us all feel like teenagers again. We were each asked to dance at one point or another by an admirer but we all declined. It was a fun-filled night with loads of special moments that we would keep close to our hearts when we go our separate ways.

THE BIG EVENT

I was awoken the next morning to the smell of festival, fried fish and freshly boiled chocolate tea. It was 0600 when I looked at the clock on my bedside table. I rubbed my eyes and thought about the day's events. First there would be the visit to the beauty salon to get my hair, manicure and pedicure done to get me properly dolled up for my big day. I wanted to let George forget about all his doubts at his first glance at me today, which is meant to be the most important and romantic day of our lives. It was 0300 when we returned from our night out and I was still tired but decided that an early start would be best since I had made special arrangements with our long time nails specialist, Denise, in order for me to go to her for 0700.

Afterwards, Althea who was a hair dresser by profession and up to recently had her own beauty shop but closed it in order to partner in her husband's food business, would take over and make me into a perfectly stunning doll. She was dressing me as well which put me right at ease knowing I was in very capable hands, hands that I could trust. She was always in charge of everyone's appearance whenever we had any family occasion. Althea had already sorted the girls' hair, as well as half of the bridal party's hair, most of my sisters' hair and of course my mother's hair, she never leaves my mother's hair to anyone else, she always has to give it that special Style's touch.

I quickly had a shower and pulled on a pair of jeans, a t-shirt and a pair of flip flops. I was careful not to put on any make up because it would only get in the way later on when as is the usual thing when you had an important event, I would be running short on time. I checked in on the girls and wrote them a quick note letting them know I was at the nails specialist and would be busy getting dressed directly afterwards so I would see them at the church. I got to the kitchen and as expected, it was my mother who was cooking up all that mouth watering food. Aware of the time that I had to leave for my appointment, she said good morning with a quick hug and kiss and pushed a small brown paper bag in my hand. As soon as I stepped into the living room to have a look at its contents I heard the tooting of a horn and knew right away it was the taxi.

The taxi was a brand new Lexus which shone in the morning's sunshine. I jumped into the back seat and said good morning to the driver who was an elderly man whom my mother often hired for transporting her when she had to go out. The car drove smoothly through the streets and I had no problem drinking my cup of chocolate tea and waxing down my fish and festival. It was exactly 0700 when I arrived at Denise's and she immediately got the operation on the way. In no time my nails were perfectly french and my feet were silky soft. I thanked her for the splendid job she had done and jumped back into the taxi which came back for me as planned and took me to the Terra Nova all suites hotel where Althea, my maid of honour Karen and Karl who is responsible for video-taping, were all waiting for me in the bridal suite.

Althea did my hair and styled it in the most extravagant style of all. She gave my hair a thorough shampoo and massaged my scalp as she went along which relaxed me initially and then woke my brain up for the day's happenings. She then blow dried my hair, straightened it and tied everything up on the very top of my head then carefully curled every strand into place all about my head. It was like artwork. She dressed me carefully in my wedding dress which she herself collected from my suitcase along with everything else that I had bought for the occasion and by the time she added my make up it looked as if it had been carefully and skilfully painted on my face. Karl started video taping me, while Karen, who was there helping out right throughout, pretended to dress me and I was looking like nothing less than a beautiful ceramic doll.

My dress was white and silky and was cut in line with the very top of my bosom, the top of my dress was hugging my body and the bottom from the waist downwards spreading outwards but not too wide and bulky and was long enough to touch the ground but not getting under foot, my trail was not too long and would be carried half the time by my maid of honour anyway. My vale was small and cute with a crown attached to the top and I wore opera length gloves which sit high on my arm between my elbow and my shoulder. By the time the limo pulled up outside, Karl got into position and I slipped on my white, two inches high, push toe, hand made, leather slippers it was exactly time to leave for the church.

In the limo I leaned my head back on the plush, comfortable seat and tried to relax but to no avail. My mind just kept going back to George's reaction to the wedding from the previous day. Was this the most important and romantic day of my life or was it the day of destruction for me like it was for Sarah, that lecturer on Campus several years earlier. We ran into a bit of unexpected traffic caused by Saturday shoppers so by the time we got to the chapel it was exactly 1125 which gave Karl only five minutes to prepare himself for the taping of the entrance of the bridal party. Meanwhile, I entered from the back with Karen in toe who saw me to the entrance and then hurried to take up her position through another side door of the church downstairs where the bridal party waited out of sight until the coast was clear at the main entrance of the chapel to march down the aisle. They left the bridal suite earlier where they were looked over by my mom, who was hard to please and she worked on them until she was happy with their appearances.

I hid away in the bridal suite which was really the church library that was temporarily set up for the purpose of the wedding. Luckily it was positioned above the main hall where everyone sat, and had a tiny window where I could see what was happening. I took a quick glance through the window and could see the Pastor, George and Paul, George's best man, who was also his best friend whom he knew for man years, standing patiently by the altar. George was dressed in his beige frockcoat suit with a white inside shirt which he had tailored for the occasion and Paul, like the grooms men wore a black tail coat suit, only more elaborate. As soon as Althea got in the door, who drove just a bit behind us and ensured I was away in the bridal suite, it was like their cue to start playing the music to start the procession.

It was the marvellous Thackeray string quartet ringing out loud throughout the Chapel and the University grounds nearby. The first pair of bridesmaid and groomsman could be seen slowly strolling down the aisle to the beat of the music, then about five seconds behind followed the next pair and so on until all five pairs of them were in one position or other along the red carpet which was laid out all the way to the altar. The bridesmaids were elegantly dressed in stylishly made, long bright-red, silk dresses which clung to their tops with a fall at the waists and sleeveless, complete with white high opera length gloves and they all looked so charming as they held their smiles and their groomsmen strolled along by their right.

It all felt so surreal as I sat and watched and wondered if it was really my wedding that everyone was participating in so well. Just before the last bridesmaid and groomsman reached the altar and fell into position then Karen followed in the same rhythmical stroll as those before her. She was well adorned in a long elegant looking floral dress, also with white opera length gloves to complete. About thirty seconds later came Cal, my handsome little nephew, who was the ring bearer. He was dressed in a white tail coat suit. As he reached the aisle he was followed by my two beautiful girls, Rosie and Melissa who were both dressed in their mini bride dresses and looked so adorable as they sprinkled both red and white rose petals from two small baskets all along the red carpet up to the altar.

At this point I heard a quick knock at the door and in came my mom. "It's time," she said hurriedly, "We should go. Are you ready?" She asked as she looked at me trying to put her finger on my mood. I stood up, giving nothing away, and she didn't push. She simply looked me over and said, "Alright, here we go." And I said. "Yes, here we go!" we went back to the limo and Karl was standing waiting for us with the door wide open and I sat down. He then proceeded to record me, posing as if I had only just arrived at the Chapel in the limo. He filmed me while I walked up to the front of the Chapel and my mom popped in her head to signal that I was ready and instantaneously "here comes the bride" by Wagner, could be heard spreading melodies in the air.

I was so nervous as I stepped in the door on my mother's arm. "This is your big day and he is the one for you, don't you ever forget that!" She had said only moments earlier, as she collected my right arm and put it through her left arm. I was wondering if I had come this far and had my entire family organize a wedding which was never meant to be. One which would see me to my very pathetic and wretched end in front of everyone I knew and held dear. I received standing ovation and everyone seemed to be in a joyous mood smiling, waving and even clapping their hands with delight, I was instantly put on the spot by this and looked up the long passage way which ended at the altar for George who glanced up at me, then turned his eyes away. I responded boldly to everyone's greeting by smiling a big bright smile which I would be expected to wear all day if there was going to indeed be a wedding and saying "Hi" in greeting to those near the end of the pew.

I saw April and Kelly who knew about George from the very beginning and their reassuring smiles gave me courage to continue all the way to the altar without faltering in self- pity and doubt and I finally felt stronger, for if they had the faith in me to come all the way from America and England respectively for my wedding then why should I not have enough faith to think it might come through. I had not completely recovered from my doubts, though I was feeling much stronger. My mom walked with me all the way to the altar as if she felt my need to lean on her. She then stopped when I was in line with George and offered my hand up to him which he took hesitantly.

As the pastor prayed he cleared his throat several times and again when the vows were said. I was so nervous when they asked me, "If I take this man to be my wedded husband". I was sure I was going to say 'no' in error because of how nervous I was. Soon it was George's turn to be asked and when asked he hesitated for a bit as if he was contemplating whether to say 'yes' or 'no'. Then, in one swift move he collected me in his arms and held me close to his face and said, "For better or worse, for richer or poorer, I George Smith take thee, my beautiful bride, Marge McFarlane, the love of my life, as my forever wife, 'til death do us part."

Everyone screamed with delight and jumped with joy. I glanced around and saw George's mom, two sisters, brother-in-law and nephews nodding their heads in agreement as if to say "typical of George". The pastor was infuriated and shouted, "Listen young man, you do not need to say anything but just give your answer 'yes' or 'no'! Do you understand?" "Oh, sorry sir, yes, I do." He said, and the pastor who was now a bit confused said, "would you like me to ask the question again?" And George said, "As you wish sir." The pastor then repeated. "Do you take this woman to be your lawfully wedded wife?" And George said, "Yes I do." And I was so happy I didn't care about the rumblings between George and the pastor because at that point the most important thing to me was that we loved each other and we did.

The pastor then looked from George to me as everyone waited in anticipation for what would come next. "You may kiss your bride." Said the pastor in a loud clear voice as if to illuminate any space for error and before he could finish George had collected me into his arms and looked me deep into my soul as he buried his lips sweetly on mine. I felt the tears coming as I responded breathlessly to his sweet hungry lips as he kissed me gently but firmly. I thought he would never let me go as he went on and on, I don't know how long we were there before he finally let me go and held his protective hands around me to steady me which he often had to do whenever we kissed while standing but peculiarly enough at this point everyone roared with laughter.

The signing of the register followed immediately after which went smoothly. As soon as the service was over we were swept away by Karl who was doing the video-taping and Wayne, the gentleman taking the pictures along with the entire bridal party. Our families had to gather around as well in order to get the family photos done first at the Chapel, then we moved further afield for the pictures of the bridal party. Karen freshened up my make up as we paraded in the Chapel gardens, Hope Gardens and Devon House taking shots of all the customary poses while video taping at the same time. Finally, we had a few shots taken at the Terra Nova Hotel. It a bright and sunny day. A beautiful day for taking pictures and we were completely posed out and hardly had a chance to exchange a word between us, George and me. We were all happy when we drove in the limo to the Terra Nova Hotel and finished off our photo shoot by having our pictures taken in front of the romantic waterfall. We then freshened up ourselves, yet again, for the reception.

As we entered the large well presented hall, George and I in front and the bridal party following in the same order as they did earlier in the Chapel. An announcement was made by the Master of Ceremony (MC), who was, no other than my charismatic, confident and multi-talented brother Sheldon. "Please put your hands together to welcome Mr. and Mrs. Smith," he requested and everyone took a break from their cocktails and hors d'oeuvres as they stood up and clapped and cheered. The room was well decorated with flowers all about and especially the podium which was packed with all kinds of colourful flowers. The tables which were covered with rich red coloured table cloths which hung all the way to the white, tiled floors were set with gold plated plates and utensils. The glasses all had George and Marge written on them with a heart between our names, down to the place name cards were professional looking. The theme of the room was red and white, which had impressive decorations all about it, it was breath-taking.

All the guests were seated and it was time to let the fun begin. George, myself and the bridal party sat on the podium where we could be seen by all the guests who stared up at us admiringly. The cake was the centre of attention which was six layers high, each one smaller than the one below it and the top one was decorated with a large six inches high ceramic bride and groom doll. It was nothing short of beautiful. So happy I was from the moment George said I do so forcefully that I did not even realize how much he clung to my hand every chance he got.

As soon as we sat down the MC started a selection of love songs which George and I had pre-selected. Songs such as, "can you feel the love tonight" by Elton John, "I'll be there for you" by Rembrandts, "it had to be you" by Harry Connick Jr, "stand by me" by Ben E. King, "tonight I celebrate my love for you" by Peabo Bryson & Roberta Flack and finally "unforgettable" by Nat "King" Cole & Natalie Cole were bellowed out in style from the sophisticated, built in, surround sound, music system. A combination of a rich Jamaican and English three course dishes were served and the different aromas were very inviting. It was the happiest day of my life. During the evening's proceedings I dedicated a poem to George which I had memorized:

On the wings of an eagle, My love for you flies.
Soaring higher and higher, And touching the skies.
I reached up above, And pulled a star from the sky.
To place it within, Your precious mind's eye.
Every time we embrace, I go to that far away place,
When we just walk hand in hand, I'm in never, never land.
Whenever I look into your eyes, I begin to get butterflies,
Then my heart skips a beat, And our lips passionately meet.
You just don't know what you have done for me, You even pushed me to the best I can be. You really are an angel sent from up above, To take care of me and shower me with love. It's so magical those things you've made, To bring back my faith that almost fade.
Now my life is a dream come true, It all began when I was loved by you.

Written by jo'Lene Tover,
Clinton Followell and an
Anonymous poet.

George in turn dedicated a speech to me within which he spoke freely and went on and on about how beautiful, wonderful, terrific, gorgeous, intelligent, precious, gracious and kind I was. He spoke with such deep emotions I thought I was going to cry, or even he would or maybe even both of us. He was so sweet, charming and sexy. I just wanted to hold him in my arms for a long, long time.

The best man's speech was done by Paul, who was both funny and entertaining and the father of the bride speech was done by my brother

Sheldon who was faced with the burden and usually tries at every family event to fill this role which he has done effectively and professionally since the death of our father. Though my brother truly shone as he addressed George's family and friends, then our family and friends so eloquently and capably and in the end thanked them for all attending and taking part in the wedding, I missed having my father there and wished he could see how happy I was on this, my most special day. I knew he would have been pleased with George like the rest of the family was.

The rest of the evening went by too quickly; I was having so much fun I never wanted the day to end. We ate our meal hungrily in between the proceedings. I had small portions of rice and peas with oxtail and jerk chicken and also potatoes with roast lamb served with sparkling red wine and George had the same for our main course. For desert I had extra smooth vanilla ice cream with cherries on top and George had cheese cake. For starter I had small slices of roast duck and George had vegetable stock soup. The food was gorgeous and we were full by the time we were finished eating.

Many of my family members and friends did precious pieces for us of songs, poems and speeches, among them was my niece Petula who could sing like a bird. She sang "when love walked in" by Thunder which was very touching. When it was time to cut the cake George and I cut the second layer together as we looked from the well decorated brightly coloured cake to each other. When we were both finished making the first cut then we cut off small pieces and fed each other for everyone to see. It was fun as I put the cake in my mouth and George bit and ate a part of it then I did the same with him. Then, I chewed a piece of cake and George kissed it along with my saliva from my mouth and then he did the same and this time I kissed it from his sweet sexy mouth. I could have done the cake feeding all day with George; I just couldn't seem to get enough.

Soon it was time for our first dance together and George held my hand and took me to the dance floor as the MC played Luther Vandross' "always & forever" and we danced to the very end before we were cheered and clapped by everyone as they had done right throughout the song. He played a host of other love songs and we danced to our hearts content. Afterwards we went around greeting everyone. It was at this point that I made arrange with April and later Kelly to see them in a few days as they would be staying on holiday for a while. I also spoke to Samantha from the RN, thanking her for making it all this way to my wedding. I was so pleased to have her. Meanwhile as we went around, George spoke to his mom, sisters and brother-in-law at length as they too would be staying in Jamaica for a brief holiday. I hugged and kissed my family members and most of my relatives and friends.

I then offered up a thank you speech, shortly after which, we made our exit to start our lives as Mr. and Mrs. Smith. We disappeared into the thicket of Terra Nova's beautiful gardens, surrounding colonial architecture which provided a lush environment for us. We held on tight to each other as we dashed off to our suite which was same place at the Terra Nova, just around the corner from where our reception was held. It was dark by then and we were desperate to be by ourselves at last. As soon as we approached the door George held me back as he said "Hold on Mrs. Smith, let me do the business." As I wondered what he was on about he swiftly picked me up and carried me a few steps in his arms, then he opened the door and walked over the threshold while he kissed me simultaneously. "Oh sweetheart, I forgot!" I said as he released me slowly.

We had a quick look around and found that our honeymoon suite had a similar theme to the reception hall; only, our suite was far more intimate. There were red and white rose petals strewn all over our suite and a double ceramic male and female attached doll with our names written across it. It was beautiful. There was a large red ribbon above our bed which read "welcome Mr. and Mrs. Smith" and I was pleased that they had cleaned and reorganized our suite since this morning when we left for the wedding in a rush.

It was also evident that my sisters had brought over our belongings and they not only packed out everything they thought we would need for the night but they also left dinner for us, just in came we didn't get a chance to eat our meal at the reception, and also a bag full with snacks. I could also see the key for the van which they left on my bed side table and a black leather case full of CD's. I took my sleek black negligee out of its pack which I bought from Victoria's Secret and went to the bathroom to freshen up and slide into it. I was proud of how my special day had turned out and looked at my radiant self in the mirror and smiled. I was happy and I was at peace with myself.

What more could I ask? "I have won yet again, the biggest hurdle of all." I thought and said a silent prayer of thanks to the Lord. I could hear George clicking away at the hotel's CD player and before long I could hear the clear sounds of Boys II Men's "I'll make love to you" and I shivered as I thought of what was to come. As I went back into the bedroom George was waiting around eagerly at the bathroom door, while he entered the bathroom I headed for our cosy bed and climbed under the covers. He quickly returned and jumped into bed beside me and collected me in his arms.

Just the touch of his hands on my body commanding his attention made me hungry for him as I looked up into his face in the very well prepared, well lit room. I heard myself groaned as he kissed me deeply, I marvelled at how I always feel I could never get enough of him and I knew instinctively that he felt the same way. He stopped for a while and just looked into my eyes; he then ran his fingers across my lips, eye brow and nose and squeezed me tight. "I love you Marge." He said and I told him I loved him in return. "Marge, you've made me a very happy man today, I thank you and I know you are the one for me." He sounded so sincere that tears brimmed in my eyes and I felt so foolish for doubting his feelings for me for even one minute. "Marge, you know I would do anything for you, I would die for you."

By that time I couldn't hold the tears back anymore. It was the wedding, everyone coming out to support us in our love and the reception, how beautifully well everything turned out and to have all my doubts washed away throughout the day and as if all that wasn't enough, now to have George tell me how much he loved me and not stopping there but to also tell me he would die for me. I knew he loved me but I just did not understand the intensity of his love. George held me tight and comforted me as I cried in his arms. I could hear Michael Bolton's voice now singing "when a man loves a woman." I shivered and cried even more while George coolly and calmly repeated, "It's alright Marge sweetheart, I didn't mean to upset you, it's alright, shhhh, it's alright." I thought about telling him how I felt last night and earlier today but I didn't want to spoil the moment nor for him to know I had doubts about how he felt after all this time so I decided to just put it out of my mind and instead comfort myself with the thought of how much he truly loved me. "I feel the same way about you." I said. "I just thought that the strength of my love for you might not be returned in the same intensity, that's all." "Oh Marge, it is returned, every bit and more." He said as he kissed the tears from my face and before I could respond he was kissing my mouth even hungrier than before.

He then removed my breasts from my negligee, squeezed them together and sucked on them as he reach down and removed my underwear with one swift pull. He then felt my wetness and was impressed by it, I could tell by his load moan and he held me even tighter as he inserted his joystick without wasting a moment. My wetness was still shivering from earlier and now I was jumping up and down with excitement. I could hear his loud groans in my ears as he moved deeper and deeper within me and his thrusts got faster and faster. He kept shouting my name in awe in a low rough voice and I kept saying, "Oh my sweet George" without even realising it at first, by the time I came to realising it I was out of control and it made me conscious of how sweet our love making was. In the background I could hear "time of my life" by Bill Medley & Jennifer Warnes. I was lost in the moment as we moved together for what seemed like an eternity, during which time things only got more and more intense and I felt myself explode just before George did with a quick deep thrust and a loud groan.

We were still clinging onto each other when we woke up to morning sounds of birds chirping and the occasional traffic humming away in the distance. I stirred as I opened my eyes to look at his handsome face and he too woke up. "You alright Marge?" he asked and before I could respond he said, "Marge, thank you for a beautiful wedding day, I love you." "Oh sweetheart, I love you too and I thank you for making my dream come through." I said. He collected me in his big arms again and just held me and kissed me. He then kissed my breasts and quickly pulled my negligee off then tasted my wetness and slid inside me while he kissed at my swollen nipples.

We woke up again just before noon and when I opened the thick drapes I could see several of the hotel guests busying themselves about the pool. We munched on some of the snacks that my sisters bought us while I reheated the rice and peas and chicken that they had also bought which I had stored away in the fridge-freezer. We ate hungrily and had a long warm bath. We then got dressed, collected our belongings and headed towards the highway, leading to el Greco in Montego Bay to begin our honeymoon. It was a quiet Sunday afternoon, the sky was blue and the sun was shining. George put a CD in the CD player and we listened in blissful peace, happy in each others silence while we looked forward to the events of the next couple of days. Tinie Tempa's "written in the stars", followed by Jessie J's "price Tag", B.O.B's "don't let me fall" and Chipmunk's "champion" followed by a host of other songs.

We stopped several times on our way in order for George to sample roast and fried breadfruit served with ackee and salt fish, okra with steamed fish, big luscious bambay and julie mangoes and so much more. We also took the opportunity to use the toilet and freshen up a few times as it was a long trip from Kingston to Montego Bay. Because we had made so many stops along the way, cruising along and enjoying ourselves it was nightfall by the time we got to Montego Bay.

WAY TO GO

We pulled into the excellent el Greco five star hotel, collected our keys and headed for our honeymoon suite, which was on two levels with the 2nd and 3rd floors overlooking doctor's cave beach in the distance. Our suite consisted of two bedrooms, 2 bathrooms, 2 baths, full kitchen, dining area, living room and balcony. It was fabulous with clear wood finish and gold plated shiny looking furniture. The walls were painted with a warm cream colour. I felt at ease when as soon as we entered our suite, we quickly filled our eyes with the attractions of our suite and the panoramic views outside our windows and balcony. Also our noses were filled with the scent of red rose petals which were strategically placed in the shape of a heart in the centre of the bed in the master bedroom.

At a closer look we saw that there was a small, red heart shaped cushion with our names on the front. Straight away I took a CD from the leather case my sisters left me the day before and placed it in the hotel's CD player, which only had various artists written on it and to my surprise the first song to play was "Everything I do I do for you", by Bryan Adams. As soon as the song started blasting out of the smooth CD surround sound music system George held my hand and pulled me down on the bed, covered me over with his body and kissed me tenderly for what seemed like hours until my lips felt sore. We were both out of breath when he stopped and by that time "Perfect love" by Trisha Yearwood was booming out of the CD player. We had another long warm bath to revive ourselves and held each other tight in the bath as we kissed and caressed each other and this time I was standing and holding onto the inside of the bath when George inserted his joy stick.

The next day we were up early as George's alarm went off at 0500 with a loud chime which was deafening. We jumped up in bed as we tried to remember why we had set the alarm in the first place. We were still tired from the previous day's trip from Kingston. Then it finally hit us that we had our island vibes cruise booked for this morning so we had to be at doctor's cave beach at 0545 for our pick up. We jumped out of bed and headed straight for the shower. We were trying to focus on what we needed to do before running off in the direction of Doctor's Cave beach but it was out of our hands as soon as we glanced at each other's nakedness.

George reached for me at the same time I started running my hands through the hair on his chest. His chest was wide and solid with the hair spiralling up and around to the left in circles, it was truly amazing to look at and to touch. I then reached down and kissed his pink nipples tenderly which turned red instantaneously. He was touching my butt by then and before long he got so excited he started rubbing my arse with a rhythmic motion and I was getting closer and closer to him due to the force of his caress. I glanced down and saw that he was hard as nails and without further ado I lifted my foot up to rest on the side of the bath and tipped up to insert George's joystick inside my increasingly hungry and hot wetness. George groaned and began to move as rhythmically as he moved his hand earlier, he then lifted me by my buttocks and held me firm so that my wetness sat directly on top of his joystick and now he was thrusting hard and deep inside me. I wrapped my legs around him as I called out his name and he groaned in response each time I called. This made me extremely horny and I started to jump and thrust my wetness against him and he got increasingly eager and anxious and thrust even quicker and deeper. The shower was pouring all over our wet steaming bodies and before long we groaned in unison with satisfaction, then George rested me down in the bath and we just cuddled each other until we recollected our strength and had a quick wash.

We dashed out of the shower and threw a few things into a bag as we quickly dressed and we were completely out of time by then so we had to literally run all the way to Doctors Cave beach. The yacht was waiting for us and we could see about twenty people on board, who all appeared to be couples and we wondered if they were on their honeymoon like we were. We quickly boarded the vessel and our journey began. We were suffering from skipping our nightly meal the night before and not be able to prepare something earlier for breakfast as we had run out of time so we went in search of some breakfast which we got without any trouble at all. A tour of the yacht was due to be given at 0615 so we had about half hour to eat. We were immediately taken to the dining room next to the galley where we could smell a waft of freshly made fruit juices, fresh tea and coffee brewing and the cooking of a variety of Jamaican cuisines.

We selected fried dumplings and callaloo cooked with salt fish and we gulped it down hungrily while we listened and rocked to Bob Marley's "three little birds", which was playing on the music system throughout the yacht. We noticed two other couples having breakfast on either side of us. The couple on the right looked locked into themselves as they sat very close to each other and spoke very softly while they stared into each other's eyes. The other couple to our left looked from us to each other with curiosity and as we glanced over at them they smiled and we knew we had found ourselves a pair of friends for our trip. The woman was tall and glamorous looking with light complexion and hanging, waist length mousy brown hair and the man who was also tall was strapping with curly dark hair. George and I decided to have a slice of orange cake and a glass of natural juice at the end of our meal and by the time we were finished it was time for our tour.

The couple to our left came over to us and introduced themselves as Reggie and Anita as they went past us on their way to the upper deck. We introduced ourselves in return and followed suit. A tall dark complexion man was introducing himself as Raymond as we approached and he went on to tell us that he was our tour guide. He then instructed us to follow him as he showed us the different rooms in the yacht. He showed us the four beautifully-appointed guest rooms, each with en-suite shower room which he informed us would accommodate up to eight members in our party, but we were not too concerned about this bit of information because we knew that by the time the yacht was back in Doctor's Cave tonight we'd be off it and back in our hotel. We wished we could have just shut everyone out of the guest room though and continue with more of what we started first thing as we got out of bed. George squeezed my hand and looked deep into my eyes as he kissed me and fingered my bra-less swollen nipples. I became aware that I was rushing so much earlier that I forgot to put my bra on. I felt ready again for George as if I could just take my clothes off right away and have him where we stood, just at the back of the small group walking through the guest room.

We became conscious that we were being watched when Raymond cleared his throat and said, "Shall we proceed?" immediately we were jolted back to reality and I felt a bit embarrassed as we shifted to let Raymond past. George was ready to sooth me with laughter as he whispered in my ear, "You think we should show him how to proceed babe?" While he teasingly and playfully undressed me. Then we were in the main salon which he supplied, will seat twelve people comfortably. This room was elegantly laid out. Next, were the three queen size stately rooms and one bunk room with two single beds which he said was ideal for any combination of families with children, couples or singles. The spacious, shaded area outside the cockpit, he informed us will seat ten at two tables, the aft deck he said also has two lounging mats for sunning and two fresh water showers for our comfort.

We spent the rest of the morning looking out at the countryside quietly by ourselves as we listened to birds chirping away and watched colourful butterflies and bees scamper from bush to bush. We saw fish of all different sizes, colours and shapes at one point or other in the clear water below the yacht. It was amazing. In the background there was always music playing quietly and now they were playing "night nurse" by Dennis Brown. We found that later on in the day, we would get a chance to learn the latest Jamaican reggae dance styles. Often, we found ourselves swaying to the rhythms of the music which would automatically lead to us touching hands, embracing, kissing and fondling each other before we are saved from ourselves by someone passing by. We went for our meal at 1200 and then realized too late that Reggie and Anita were having theirs at 1300. The group was split into two for meals because there wasn't enough room to seat everyone for meals at once. As we looked at our menus, we were impressed by how much there was to choose from. From a selection of roast: yams, potatoes and breadfruit to boiled: bananas, dumplings, and rice for staples. Served with; escovitch fish, roast: chicken, beef and pork, (oxtail, barbeque chicken and curried goat). George chose roast chicken with roast potatoes and I chose a combination of barbeque chicken and curried goat with boiled rice. The food was delicious and while we ate we stopped for a moment and held hands across the table. We looked deep into each others eyes as we listened tenderly to "number one" by Gregory Isaacs. We could feel the yacht below us moving ever so slowly and at times it would stop briefly during our venture out across the flat, calm waters of a blue-green bay. We were having a great time aboard this luxury yacht which would eventually take us to Magaritaville in Negril, then back to our hotel in Montego Bay.

After lunch we went out to where most people were as they gathered around Raymond, listening to his guided tour while the music continued to play softly in the background. We listened for a few minutes as he talked about the history of Montego Bay before we were enticed back into being by ourselves again and like teenagers with hormones flying about, out of control, we started to pace about the yacht hoping to find somewhere where we could be alone. When we made our yacht booking we did not think that we would be in a position where we would need a room so badly but now that we were on the yacht and all the rooms on board were all occupied we wished we had made other arrangements.

We went from the cockpit to the main salon and at one point when we thought we had got lucky and George was putting his hand up my short skirt into my silk knickers and thrusting his finger deep inside my wetness while he sucked on my swollen nipples hungrily we were definitely caught out. We didn't hear him coming but one of the galley chefs came right upon us as I was purring in agony and we could tell that he was just as startled as we were as we jumped away from each other and quickly went back to the upper deck. We went back to our little corner where we spent most of the morning and talked about the dates we have been on and how we felt about each other at the time to try and alleviate some of the strong urges we were feeling for each other.

Before long we were up in each others arms kissing and falling all over each other as we listened to "reggae love song riddim" by Turbulance Chuck Fenda, Tarrus Riley and Sanchez. Reggie and Anita came over briefly to where we were hanging out and we learnt that they were from California in the United States and that they themselves were on their honeymoon. We were happy to learn that there were other honeymooners amongst us. We decided it would be a good idea to have a drink with them later on when we got to Jimmy's Buffet in Margaritaville. Later on when we invited them, they were pleased with the idea and said they were more than happy to join us. At 1500 we went back to where Raymond was and the now very small crowd of men and women circling him and waited for the reggae dance lessons to begin.

A few moments later as everyone down below was making their way back to the upper deck, Raymond announced that the reggae dancing lessons were to be held in the dining room where there was adequate deck area and he signalled to us to follow him. When we got to the dining room, the selection of the music quickly changed and we could now hear Mavado's "don't wanna be a memory", "dem a talk" and "pepper", followed by "frenzy" by Sanchez, "make money" by Serani and more. Two of the many dances he demonstrated to us were "skip to malloo" and "parra-die". It was quite a sight with everyone on board seeming like such amateurs at reggae/dancehall dancing that it would have taken a life-time for Raymond to successfully teach any of the dances to them. Our new found friends Anita and Reggie came close to catching some of the dances but they lacked the confidence that is an essential element to performing any dance.

It was awesome when we arrived at Jimmy's Buffet. The sun was shining bright but the day was cool and the sky was clear and blue. The beach was a beautiful light blue and the sand was pearly white and soft. I took off my sandals and George took them from my hands as we strolled along the beach on the sand nearby, hand in hand. It was ever so soothing. We could hear Shaggy's "Feel the rush" playing and George took me in his arms and kissed me tenderly. We then chose a set of chairs that were near to the bar with umbrellas above them. We drank a few pina colada's and a margarita each over our evening meal. They had a variety of dishes and I chose rice and peas and oxtail while George chose rice and peas and barbeque chicken. Anita and Reggie joined us as planned when we first sat down and we bought them a couple of rounds of drink and they returned the favour.

We were nice and tipsy by the time we returned to the yacht. It was past twilight and nothing could be seen by natural light. We went back to where we sat on the upper deck which now had dim lighting but almost everyone else escaped to the safety of down below as the yacht was moving much faster now compared to the snail pace which was employed earlier. George and I were enjoying the ride as we held onto each other and cuddled and kissed continuously. They were playing a combination of Gregory Isaac's and Dennis Brown's love songs now and the entire setting was very romantic.

There were so many times we wanted to just strip down and make passionate love to each other but we held out, though it took all our strength. We had a brilliant time on the yacht but it was a relief when we finally got back to our suite at the hotel and climbed into bed together. We quickly stripped each other clothes off and that was all we could bear after the long wait all day. Without further ado George inserted his joystick. His thrusts were deeper and more powerful than ever while he held my buttocks against him firmly. He was thrusting even deeper and very fast now as he sucked my breasts in his sweet mouth and all I could do was scream and groan in ecstasy. George thrust a final hard thrust and we both groaned in unison.

We awoke to the sound of my alarm and we jumped up startled with pounding headaches, it was 0530. We had no time to spear so we hurriedly leapt into the shower together and had a quick wash while we tried our best to ignore our headaches. We jumped on the bus which awaited us at the front of the hotel at 0600 and were on our way. When we got to the main road it was still dark and the streets were empty except for a few people busying about on their way to work. The air was just a bit cool and we could smell the salt from the sea. It wasn't long before our headaches subsided and we started feeling hungry so we scuffed some chicken and vegetable sandwiches we grabbed from the fridge in our dining room on our way out of our suite. It was bright out and the terrain was mountainous when we got to Croydon Plantation which is a working coffee and pineapple plantation located at the base of the Catadupa Mountains. We were allowed to sample several delicious tropical and exotic fruits including pineapple, banana, sugar cane and jackfruit fresh from the grounds.

The view was picturesque with lush vegetation, wild flowers in abundance and beautiful waterfalls. There were times when George and I lost ourselves amongst the bushes for a chance to fondle and kiss each other then we'd catch up with the tour guide without anyone missing us. After a while, he took us to the coffee groves and showed us how coffee is produced as well as some of their other produce. He also gave us the history behind the plantation. The atmosphere was tranquil and everything about the plantation was breath- taking. Before we knew it, it was noon and time for our delicious Jamaican lunch which was provided at the top of the rolling mountains under a covered pavilion. We had barbeque chicken with rice and peas and washed it down with natural pineapple juice. We then sipped our Blue Mountain Coffee slowly, enjoying the rich aroma. The trip served to refresh and revive us from the night before and we were fascinated by all the new information we had gained. George and I bought a couple of packets of coffee to take back with us as gifts for friends and relatives.

We returned to el Greco early in the afternoon and headed straight to the hotel's restaurant for our meeting with my sister April and her partner Tyrone and also Kelly and her husband Charles which we had arranged earlier. The two couples knew of each other for several years but had not met until the day of the wedding. Nonetheless, they found each other and were now sitting together exchanging stories about their holidays. They were happy to see us and it was nice to have some familiar company for a change. We told them about our trip to Negril aboard the yacht and our time at the plantation earlier then we discussed with them over a drink what we were doing for the next few days. April and Tyrone were staying at the luxurious Marriott hotel and Kelly and Charles at Sandals.

It was a very warm afternoon and we could see the beautiful Doctor's Cave beach down below with a colourful array of beach umbrellas all about and loads of beach bums moving about. We felt a bit envious of all those people parading around in bathing suits of all make, colours and sizes and had grown bored with just sitting in at the restaurant, though there were so many attractive dishes on the menu. We decided that we would go for a swim at the beach and return to the restaurant later for our evening meal.

April, Kelly and I used the master suite and the males used the second bedroom while we changed into our swimming gears. I put on my two piece, skimpily cut, shocking green colour bathing suit which looked great because I was fit and in great shape. April wore a blue two piece bathing suit which showed off her wide hips and Kelly wore a low cut top showing off her boobs and a bikini bottom both gold and black in colour. George wore a black bathing trunk which made him looked very muscular and sexy, while Tyrone and Charles wore blue and grey trunks respectively that made them look very smart. The three of us wrapped ourselves in our big white fluffy beach towels and all six of us wore our flip flops and we joked and laughed with each other as we quickly made our escape, eager to get to the sun and the fun at Doctor's Cave beach.

It was terrific as we bathed, played with a big yellow beach ball in the water that we took with us and sat in the sand gossiping over a couple of drinks. It was nightfall when we all went back to our honeymoon suite and changed for our evening meal. For the fun of it, we each ordered something we liked then we shared it among the group of us and by doing that we all ended up sampling six different dishes for our main course which were a combination of Jamaican and English dishes. The food was delicious, the service great and the atmosphere romantic. It was marvellous. George and I finally hugged them goodbye and saw the pair of them off in a black taxi. We were satisfied that it had turned out to be a fabulous reunion. We slowly walked back to our suite holding hands, feeling happy and contented.

When we got back to our suite, I decided it was time that I made George truly mine by giving him a little something to remember our honeymoon by that he would never be able to forget for the rest of his life. I had just got out of the shower with a large thick white towel wrapped around me. I took out a new lingerie I had bought on the internet specifically for this purpose. It was a bra like silky, golden top which exposed my cleavage and a very short pair of shorts like nickers to match which sat very well on my butt but at the same time exposing the jaws of my buttocks. Also in the pack was a pair of very thin, transparent stockings and matching gloves which go all the way up to my elbow from my middle finger with gold glitter all over them. I left my hair to fall about my shoulders with my face properly made-up as I got dressed with my high heels, knee high boots which were black and sleek to finish. I was looking very attractive but at the same time a bit street (hard corp).

I took out a CD from my hand bag which I had purchased on line. It was a mixed take and I had personally hand picked the songs chiefly for this purpose which were only a few but containing very powerful lyrics. The songs in the order that they appeared on the tape for special effects were:

1. Only girl in the world by Rihanna
2. What we gonna do by H2O ft. Platinum
3. Drop it like it's hot by Snoop Dogg ft. Pharrel
4. Turn me on by Kevin Lyttle
5. Temperature by Sean Paul
6. Smack that by Akon ft. Eminem
7. Never believe you by Mavado
8. Hold you by Gyptian
9. King of the dancehall by Beanie Man
10. Batty Rider by Buju Banton
11. Dutty Wine by Tony Matterhorn

The main light in the room was on which made it look very bright and I pulled the arm chair from the corner and put it to stand in the middle of the room. I then popped the CD into the CD player which was on the bedside table and stood next to it. As soon as George stepped out of the shower and into our room I pressed play and Rihanna's voice came through clearly. I could see him literally step back with his eyes popped wide open. I could tell he was shocked and I was glad for that response because it would keep him on his toes for what I was about to do. I did not smile but looked him straight in his eyes and held his attention.

I motioned to him to sit on the chair and he did so without question and I felt as though I was a school teacher giving orders to a child. I then went into the open space in our room in front of where he sat on the chair and he kept his eyes on me as I danced to the songs as appropriate. He made several attempts to kiss and cuddle me and I had to stand strong in order to not defeat the purpose of my objective. After all, I had gone to a lot of trouble.

By the time Beanie Man's "batty rider" was playing my sweetheart couldn't take it anymore and I felt the same way but I didn't come this far to fail so I continued, only this time I didn't motion him back to the chair but instead let him stay by me and rubbed and wined on him. I could see how much he was enjoying it, plus he just kept marvelling at my every move which made me want to please him more and more.

When Tony Matterhorn's "dutty wine" started playing he dragged me over to the chair where he was sitting and was trying to take my clothes off. I was pleased it was the last song because I didn't want to go on anymore. I just wanted to be with my husband. By the time the chorus started he had succeeded in shifting my knickers and putting his joystick into my wetness. I was sitting on his joystick now as he sat on the chair and I was doing the 'dutty wine' with my arse on his lap and my hands on the floor. It was not exactly how I planned it but it worked well so I just went with it. I was twisting my head around in circles while my hair fell all about my head and face and I can't remember ever feeling as horny as I was feeling now.

By the time the song finished I had no excuse to be dancing anymore so I allowed George to lift me and take me to the bed where we pleasured each other for hours on end as we exploded again and again in each others arms before falling asleep breathless and nockered, clinging on to each other.

The next day we were weeping tired but we both loved a good adventure and wanted to make the most of our honeymoon by filling it with memories so we were adamant not to take a day off to spend indoors just yet. We were again startled by the big blasting noise the alarm made when it brought us out of our blissful sleep and to our feet at 0600. We barely had enough time to shower before I dived into the fridge for two cheese and tomato sandwiches and chucked them in my knap sack.

The fresh sea air was nice and cool as it blew against our faces and the morning was bright. We ran to the front of the hotel and this time it was a large air conditioned Juta bus which we embarked in and quickly dashed for the back seat which was both private and comfortable. The bus ride gave us a varying view of different lifestyles in the urban communities from Montego Bay to Negril as we headed for Rick's Café cruise. On our arrival we boarded a cosy boat and went on a very enjoyable excursion.

We departed Negril to cruise to spectacular reefs in Negril Marine

Park and we got the opportunity to jump into the deliciously warm water for some snorkelling. It took us a while to get our gear on and we adopted the buddy system in order to ensure each others safety but once we hit the water it was all good fun and game. The coral reefs were pristine up close. It was breath-taking and George kept close to me not letting me out of his sight while we were down below.

When we returned to the boat it took us all the way to the West End along the coastline in a slow cruising motion while we sipped diluted Jamaica rum. Cruising back to Negril as the sunset, we decided to change over to drinking fruit punch. We could see the view of a group of merry-makers on a boat from the Hedo, which was entertaining. At Rick's Café we watched the cliff jumping for a bit which were mainly local professional males jumping from high up to many feet down below.

Occasionally one or two brave tourist would join in and watching them jump was quite nerve wrecking. There was reggae music playing and "stir it up" by Bob Marley was ringing out in the evening air. George held my hand and squeezed it as we watched the beautiful sunset. We had a delicious roast chicken and roast yam meal and danced to the music until about 2000 when it was time to board our bus back to el Greco. When we returned to our suite, as soon as we closed the door behind us we reached for each other.

The events of the day had made us hungry for each other and we didn't need much preparation so after a quick, deep kiss I reached down and licked and sucked at George's nipples as he caressed my breasts and felt my wetness. He then quickly licked at my wetness and put his joystick in. we were so eager, we both thrust our hips towards each other and held on tight as we groaned passionately. We couldn't wait. So sweet it was as our thrusts got quicker and quicker as we pleasured each other that I felt like crying and George who was watching my face in the dim light, held onto me even tighter and kissed my lips slowly and tenderly as he peered into my soul, uncovering every detail.

At this point I tried to control the tears but I couldn't and they rolled down my face onto my cheeks. George looked at me with such tenderness and I could sense him blaming himself but my hips were still pushing up rhythmically against him hungrily and he couldn't resist seeking to satisfy his unbearable hunger. By now I was weeping uncontrollably and I felt so odd because I couldn't put my finger on it. I knew that I was enjoying our love making enough to make me want to cry blissfully but that wasn't it. It was something else but I couldn't figure it out. Without warning we jerked one final jerk and exploded in ecstasy. George looked a bit worried as we lay there looking at each other and holding onto to each other but instead of saying anything he just rubbed my back and kissed away my tears before kissing me tenderly for a long, long time.

We were up at the crack of dawn again the next day and were rushed as usual to get to our bus on time. We filled our eyes with the beautiful scenery on our way to Dunn's River Falls. It was glorious when we got to Dunn's River Falls which offers up a lot of panoramic views. We were determined to climb the falls by ourselves without a guide, which we did successfully, holding onto each other every step of the way. Each time I slipped or tripped George was ever so worried that it made me feel so guilty for worrying him so. Whenever he tripped I prayed to God each time to spear my husband. There were times when I would look at him as we climbed and I would wonder if I could possibly love him anymore than I already did. I loved him so much. It took us a great deal of time and effort and even skill to climb the falls and when we were finished we were exhausted. We took a break to get our breath back and went for a swim in the adjoining beach nearby.

At lunchtime we bought rice and peas, steam parrot fish and a long drink of refreshing, natural, orange juice from one of the shops nearby. We found a cosy, shaded spot under a tree near the beach and we hugged and kissed playfully as we talked and joked with each other. Not long after we went horse riding on the beach. It was like a dream come through. I enjoyed the strong feel of the horse moving below me as we set off on a slow and steady, lengthy walk. We decided on one horse for both of us because we did not want to be apart. Even though George was a very talented rider, I was a novice and he did not want to take any chances with me riding by myself. We held onto each other as we rode and I leaned against him for support as I sat behind him. He led the horse carefully and professionally and I felt confident that I was in safe hands.

As we headed off to Draux Hall to return the horse where we had collected it earlier, we saw loads of opportunities to play around on empty sections of the beach and in country bushes near Draux Hall but our disciplined nature was in control and we almost got away unscathed, back to the beach in a taxi having done little more than kissing and caressing each other. Except for the one time as we strolled through the bushes, the steady motion of the horse riding while I was sitting up close against George's firm bottom made me so horny that I rested my hand up against his trousers and started stroking his joystick without even realizing it until George started to groan with delight. I quickly removed my hand and apologised without thinking and George begged me not to apologise but instead dismounted, tied the horse to a tree and started licking at my wetness as I was sat on the horse. I couldn't believe the rush I felt.

He then shoved his long, thick finger deep inside my wetness and as I began to shirk and purr softly he begged me to let him go on stroking me. My pelvis started gyrating in quick successions and I could see George smile with pleasure as he took my hand, bringing it to rest on his trousers front again and told me to play with it. I did as my husband told me without question and he held onto me with his strong arms and put me to lean against his hard, strong body. He then lifted my left foot, put it up on his and anxiously took out his joystick. He opened his legs, leaned back on the tree and thrust his joystick deep within me. It was the sweetest thing ever. I purred with excitement, wanting more and more. I could hear George growling with delight. "Oh my sweet George!" I started whispering and he smiled down at me with pride. We were in our embrace for quite a while before we exploded like a burst reservoir with loud passionate screams. George took me in his arms and said "Marge, I have never had anyone in my life like you before, you are the best thing that ever happened to me and I love you with all my heart."

He then kissed me deeply and attempted to put his joystick into my wetness again but we heard foot steps close by and hurriedly picked up our clothes from the ground where we had taken them off in the rush, letting them fall without a care. We dressed quickly, released the horse and were back on our way again. When we got back to Dunn's River it was time to leave and everyone was already seated in the bus. We hopped back on board and recounted our exciting adventure while we travelled back.

When we got back, we went to our suite and went for a warm, strawberry scented bath. I put the thick red candles at strategic points all around the bathroom and they were letting off red berry scent. The two scents together created a sweet aroma and after a long soak cuddling and kissing each other George kissed my wetness and I kissed and licked his joystick. We pleasured each other for a long time as we relaxed, letting the warm water and the romantic atmosphere of the bath soothe our bodies. George then rested me against the tiled wall at the bottom of the bath and held me firmly up against it, then, he shoved his joystick deep inside me, taking me from behind. At the same time he caressed my swollen nipples, kissed my lips and fingered my clit.

He then swiftly picked me up and placed me in our bed where he turned my back to him with one of his feet between mine then he inserted his joystick and pumped deep inside me. He had put in a CD when we came in and Brandy's "die without you" was playing now. By the time we cried out together, overjoyed, it was 2130. We decided to call for room service to provide us with our evening meal. I had stir fried chicken and rice and peas and George had stewed chicken and rice and peas for our main course. We laid about our suite after our meal enjoying our time alone and getting organized and rested for the next day but at about 2230 George pulled me into bed again. I thought we were having an early night but to my surprise he was undoing my black and pink negligee I had just proudly put on and was throwing the bits about the room, then when he was satisfied that all the pieces were off he took me into his embrace and kissed my lips, my swollen tender nipples and my wetness. He then placed his joystick inside me and in no time I was humping him right back as if I hadn't had any all day long. I marvelled at how he can make me ready for him at the drop of a hat. When we finally exploded in each others arms, George reached for me again and again that night into the wee hours of the morning.

The next morning we were not up too early. We woke up naturally to the chirping of birds and the rushing of the sea. Also, we could hear the splashing of the pool as early morning swimmers took their dip. I looked up at the clock on my bedside table, it was 0630. I shifted in George's embrace and went back to sleep. When we finally crawled out of bed it was 0830. We had our shower together and kissed and caressed each other as we stood under the brisk, heavy flow of the warm water. We dressed and strolled across to the restaurant where we had ackee, salt fish and fried dumplings for breakfast. George rubbed his leg against mine underneath the table as we sipped our tea, then he reached down his right hand and massaged the inside of my leg all the way up to my wetness.

I quickly looked around at the other customers to see if they could tell what we were doing but realized that they were taking no notice of us. He thrust his middle finger in and out of my wetness as I thrust my front towards his hand repeatedly and when the waitress came over to ask if we wanted anything else we knew we had to give it up and be on our way. We knew it was almost time for our river rafting anyway so though we wanted desperately to go back to our room and get it on with each other we had to just abort the idea completely. As we glanced at our watches we knew that all we had time for now was to grab our bags and be on our way. When we got to Doctor's Cave beach the tour guide, John was already there waiting for us so we carefully climbed aboard and made ourselves comfortable.

On our way out as we drifted along, John told us all about the history of Montego Bay and we listened dreamily as the raft shifted backwards and forwards in a jerky motion. We could hear John now but we knew it wouldn't be for very much longer as he proceeded: - "Montego Bay is the second city of Jamaica, and the capital of the parish of St. James. This city has a long history, which started with the settlement of the Spanish to Montego Bay after 1510.The reason the Spanish had named the city 'Bahia de Mantega' was because of the huge quantities of pig fat they found here, and which they had started exploring the South American and West Indian colonies. It was after the British occupation of Jamaica in 1655…" But before long we were completely dazed. We just sat together holding each other while we drifted cosily.

At times we were awoken by someone asking a question of John or someone along the beach talking loudly as we passed. The sights were beautiful and the weather brilliant. It was lunch time when we returned and we headed back to the restaurant at el Greco. This time we had roast potatoes and curried goat. Then we headed back to our room to finish what we started earlier. That afternoon we decided we could now afford to spend the rest of our honeymoon kicking back and enjoying the inclusivity of the hotel. The next morning we slept until we were satisfied then we showered, had breakfast, and went to the gym. We then went to the pool after lunch and back to our suite to pleasure each other for glorious hours without the need to rush off anywhere. In the evenings we dressed in our best gears and were entertained by the live performances at the hotel.

On our last morning at the hotel before check out at noon we got up at 0700. We went to the restaurant for our last breakfast and we knew that we were going to miss the hotel that we had so enjoyed spending our time at for several days now. In a way we were glad to be leaving because we were so aware of how much the girls were missing us so we headed back to Kingston to spend time with them, visit with a few relatives and to say our farewell.

SAYING GOODBYE

Now our honeymoon was over and all in all we had a terrific time. I hadn't seen a lot of my relatives and friends who were present at the wedding for a long time. We decided to visit a few of them, though we had very little time left but we were aware that it might be a while yet before we returned to Jamaica. On our way back from Montego Bay we took the opportunity to pop in to see my siblings along the way in order to say goodbye since we were leaving in a few days.

We stopped at my sister, Stacey's in Montego Bay and we stayed for a few minutes. We briefly recounted what we got up to on our honeymoon and she gave us loads of fresh provisions which came directly from her father-in-law's farm. The plan was that our mom would cook and freeze them for us to take back with us. We bid all four of them good bye and proceeded towards Old Harbour in order to say Good bye to my brother Sheldon and his wife Beth. We also took the opportunity while we were there to freshen up and have a nice cup of tea after the lengthy journey from Montego Bay.

Sheldon and Beth gave us fresh tomato and gungo peas which they grew in their own back yard. We went to Vicky's next who gave us a proper, cooked meal and we quickly went over to see Trudy and Nick. Vicky gave us fresh mangoes, some of which we decided we would enjoy while we were still in Jamaica as they we so enticing. The next stop was in Greater Portmore where we saw Althea and her kids at the house and then after a brief rest she took us over to the shop where Jeff was working. She gave us loads of snacks that we could take with us for the children to have while we travel back. When we finally reached Payton Place it was nightfall and the children were very happy to see us. We hugged and kissed them and saw them to bed with loads of plans which would all include them for the next few days.

The next morning we were up at 0630. George gave my mom a hand preparing breakfast while I saw to the girls. After they were bathed and dressed, Melissa in an adorable pink pants and blouse to match while Rosie wore blue jeans with a floral blouse. We all sat down and had our breakfast while we went over what we had planned for the day. "Mom, you can come with us if you'd like." I said but my mom was quick to decline saying she had a lot to do that day and I suspected she didn't want to impose because she felt we needed time alone with the children in order to catch up on what they got up to while we were away. I appreciated her concern and gave her a grateful look across the table. After breakfast she took the children to the living room where she turned on the television for Melissa to watch cartoons while she engaged Rosie in a game of snake and ladder. As George and I had our shower and got dressed we could hear them talking and laughing with each other.

We headed out at 0730. It was a bright and sunny day and the morning air was fresh and crisp. We could see a few students with their knap sack on their backs and some with their large UWI folders up against their breasts, on their way to their lectures or the library to work on various projects and assignments. I was a bit nostalgic as memories of my university days came flooding back to me and I briefly relived the countless lectures and tutorials which I attended and the numerous exams which I sat. "It was not an easy time." I said to myself shaking my head. "What is it Marge?" said George, as he looked at me with concern in his eyes and I told him about some of the lectures which I attended. Some of which were boring and were it not for the exams which followed you would happily skip them.

There were other lectures which were so touching that you would brush at a few tears. I can remember this handsome, brilliant, young Economics lecturer, whom I will never forget. He was great right throughout the semester and he always made sure that he got through to all of his students but one day near to the end of the semester he gave us his last lecture and apologised saying that he didn't want to fail us and his country but he just couldn't live in Jamaica anymore. He said he had witnessed an ordeal while he was with his partner as they travelled in their car one day and he felt he couldn't do anything about it and that he couldn't live in that way. His story was very touching and we could see that he was close to tears as he tried to tell us as much as he could but he couldn't disclose too much.

Also, there was this Abnormal Psycholoogy lecture I had which was given by a lecturer who had just joined us from the United States and she told us of a woman who while she was pregnant she would become ill with borderline personality disorder and would sit and eat an entire chicken uncooked. She even showed us pictures of the woman eating the raw chicken which was pretty disturbing. There were other times of course when you had such fun filled lectures you just had to laugh out loud. There was this brilliant lecturer who taught us Dancehall Culture and even if initially you didn't have an appreciation for the music, the dance and the whole culture surrounding the dancehall, by the time he was done with you, you would be doing the butterfly, pon di river, parachute or even the dutty wine. He would even demonstrate to us during his lectures how to do these dances and he was an extremely good dancer who just knows how to entertain others and have great fun himself.

Most of the lectures though leave you dumb struck with new knowledge and information. Tutorials were always mind blowing whenever it was your turn to do your presentation, especially if it was a large group. The exams were always nerve wrecking. What really helped me though was the fact that I lived so close to the campus so whenever I felt wounded or overwhelmed I would just go home to my family, to a different kind of reality. It was 0800 when we got to the Bob Marley museum on Hope Road which is about three miles from Payton Place but because of the congestion within that vicinity during peak hours with students and staff travelling to the University and the various high and primary/preparatory schools and offices in the region what would have normally been a fifteen minutes drive took twice that time.

The museum is what used to be Bob Marley's home which had a huge metal gate and high walls surrounding it. We were given a tour of the museum which was very interesting, made me feel closer and brought me more in touch with the memories I have of the legend. Later on we watched a movie about Bob Marley's life which span from 1945-1981. He was born as Robert Nesta Marley on February 6, 1945 in Nine Miles, St. Ann, Jamaica. His mother was an 18 year old Jamaican woman, Cedella Booker while his father was a 50 year old English captain named Norval Sinclair Marley, who was stationed in Jamaica. Bob and his mom moved to Kingston, the capital of Jamaica during his teen years to settle in Trench Town, Kingston. Bob experienced a childhood filled with poverty and violence. After attending the Stepney School in Kingston, Bob spent some time acquiring a trade as a welder.

During his youth, Bob developed a love for singing early on through his involvement in the church choir and the encouragement from friend Desmond Dekker. It went on to show us his progress throughout his musical career, his close brush with death and finally his early death. Afterwards we returned home to a delicious meal consisting of salt mackerel, dumplings and bananas which my mom prepared and in no time our plates were cleaned. George cleared up while my mom and I took the children into the big back yard where they pranced about teasing and playing with each other.

I told my mom about our plans in the next few days to take the children to Devon House and Rockfort Mineral Baths and that we would like for her to come along to spend time with us and the children and she refused at first but then eventually agreed saying that it might be a good idea for her to get out of the house and also to spend some time with us as we would be leaving soon. In the evening we took the children for ice cream in Liguanea which they got on cones then we went for a walk at Sovereign Centre and they buzzed about hopping and skipping from store to store. When we got back it was their bedtime and George and I read them a story and tucked them into bed. George, mom and I stayed up until late that night catching up and drinking sorrel (A Jamaican drink which is customarily drank at Christmas) which my mom had saved for us.

The next morning we were up at 0700 and after breakfast we all climbed into the van and went on our way to Devon House where George and I went to earlier, on the eve of our wedding day. Devon House is a restored great house in the heart of New Kingston which is near the Terra Nova Hotel. We went on a tour of the great house and went from the master bedroom, the sewing room, the illegal gaming room upstairs whose stairs are hidden in the ceiling and the sunny ballroom with relief ceiling, which still had the original chandelier and an English piano. The tour guide told us that the historic structure is filled with antiques and antique reproductions from 1880's which were done by Things Jamaican. After the tour we walked along the full length of the grounds as we filled our eyes with the beautiful scenery all about and the brightly coloured flowers of every kind. It was amazing and the children loved it. We bought rice and peas and baked chicken for lunch on the premises and we sat in the van until we were finished eating.

We then took the opportunity to look at and closely examine the items on display at the souvenir and gift shops and we marvelled at how much skill and patience was employed in the making of most if not all of the products which were work of art. When we were satisfied and had bought some very special pieces which were irresistible to us, we went back out to the gardens and sat on the concrete benches facing Hope Road as we watched both people and traffic go by. We bought a variety of snacks for the children upon their requests which were roughly every half hour.

On our way back to Payton Place we went to August Town to visit my mother's sister. As we drove through August Town, memories of Silver Hawk sound system and the few times I attended the dances came flooding back to me. My sister Althea and Becky, a friend we were very close to when we were growing up, were pro's at the dances. They would always dress in the latest fashion and always knew all the latest dance moves. Little stars they were. My mom was happy for the chance to see her sister, Nena whom she hadn't seen for a while and they embraced each other and became locked into a lengthy conversation as soon as she came to the gate to receive us. She was hospitable to us as always and I tried to lock certain features of her into my memory because I knew it would be a while again before I would see her next.

We saw some of my cousins while we were there and we talked about past evens and catch up with current happenings. They were glad to meet George and Melissa and even though they already knew Rosie, they were surprised at how much she had grown. We saw the girls off to bed when we got back and afterwards mom took out the family photo albums which she shared with George and we laughed and talked into the wee hours of the morning. Mom was happy for our company and we were more than happy to be able to spend time with her because during my years in the Navy and even now that I am no longer in the Navy I rarely ever get to see her or even worse, spend time with her, which I missed.

Splash, splash went the water as we moved about playfully at the Rockfort Mineral Baths. We made a small circle, the four of us as George held Melissa in his hands. George and I wore the same bathing gear which we wore while we were in Montego Bay and my mom and the children all wore one piece bathing suits. I always admire my mom's ability to look youthful, fresh and trendy and the fact that nobody could tell her real age just by looking. Whenever we took our mom shopping or shopped for her whether locally or overseas we always get her the latest and trendiest which she loves. I look at her now from her bluntly cut and brightly coloured hair to her shapely bowed legs and I knew she would be with us for a very long time to come.

I was glad that though she was still faithful to my father even after his death that she wasn't in a rush to join him where he was laid to rest at Dovecot Memorial Park, just a few feet away from my brother, Agustus who was laid to rest a few years earlier. Also, laid to rest at Dovecot are my sister, Adalia who died recently and my very young niece, Simone, (Vicky's daughter) several years ago. My parents were definitely in love. They were married for more than fifty years when my father passed away. He was a very proud man who worked hard every day of his life. He was a respectable man and very courageous as well.

My father was tall, dark and slim with a jovial nature, while my mother is full bodied, short and of light complexion. Ever since I can remember my mom has always been very attractive, even when I was a little girl I was consciously aware of this. George excused himself from the bath and returned a few minutes later with a big colourful beach ball which we used to play 'catching' in the water. The water was a bit cool but the sun was warm so we felt comfortable. The children requested snacks on several occasions which I went and got for them. Mom spread the blue picnic blanket out on the green luscious grass and we sat in the sun and ate the mouth watering run dung, dumplings and green bananas which my mom prepared that morning for our trip.

After sucking up some sun in our systems we couldn't resist going back into the cool water. We bathed until late in the evening. We had an excellent time in the warm sun with the cool water about us. On our way back and not without some resistance from my mom, we stopped in Liguanea at North Side plaza and bought pan chicken which was well seasoned, hot and very tasty. When we finally got back George and I saw the girls off to bed while mom made us a quick snack, then the three of us took up our positions on the sofa which was becoming a tradition for us. We then recapped the day's events with laughter while we looked at the news on the television.

Afterwards we went through the honeymoon pictures which we had printed at the photo studio and collected as we went past Liguanea that morning. There were loads of pictures and my mom had something to say about each of them as she looked at it closely. For each picture, we explained to her what was happening in the background, recreating the moments for her and reliving them with her. She loved it and we enjoyed sharing it all with her. It was great to have someone who was interested in us enough to do this with us. We then discussed what was on the agenda for the following day and we could see that my mom wasn't too happy about what was coming next. It was another late night for us and we helped mom to clear away the tea cups and the small dishes which we had the orange cake from earlier, then we said good night and were off to bed.

We woke up at 0800 and felt rested for a change which was good because we had a hectic day ahead of us. We took our time in getting ready for the day and by the time we left our bedroom the girls were up. I saw to their bath then we sat down to breakfast. Mom had made corned meal porridge, fried dumplings and ackee and salt fish. We ate greedily as we looked forward to what was in store for us. After breakfast, mom played snakes and ladder with Rosie as she cuddled Melissa on her lap who was watching cartoons and babbling along with the programme. George and I packed our belongings in our suitcases quietly, conscious of how much we would miss my mom, the sun, the sand and the beautiful island. We didn't realize how much packing we had to do which were mostly our wedding gifts which had to be carefully wrapped up in bubble wrap padding to ensure that they didn't get damaged during transit. We were amazed at how many gifts we got from our relatives and friends. We had to leave most of them behind which we would later make arrangements to have shipped to us. We also gave mom whatever she would have.

We stopped for lunch at 1200 and ate the sprat fish and festivals which my mom made earlier. After lunch we carried on with our packing. This time it was mainly the souvenirs we bought and those special items we had acquired during our stay which we packed safely in bubble wrap and secured with masking tape. Finally, I took out the DVD of our wedding which mom had received earlier in the mail and had tucked it away in our chest of drawers. I then saved the DVD to my laptop and attached it to our email accounts which we sent to all our siblings and George's mom's email accounts. We then scanned our wedding pictures which were of a very high quality and sent them out as well. Afterwards, we sat down with mom and the kids and watched the DVD. We were amazed at its high quality which we thought was just like watching a high definition film.

We had our chicken and boiled rice and gungo peas for our evening meal a bit early at 1600. My brother Phillip came by shortly afterwards to see us off and he gave George a hand packing our luggage in the van while I dressed the girls for our flight. After we said our goodbye to him George and I dressed and finished just in time for Amanda's arrival. Mom gave us some frozen ackees, tastee patties and all the food from my siblings which she had pre-prepared which we placed in our hand luggage along with some snacks for our journey. Then we all climbed into the van. Amanda and mom sat directly behind us while the two girls sat next to each other behind them and our luggage was neatly placed in the back seat.

I glanced at a familiar looking vendor on the Campus as we went past and I remembered how much I used to be motivated by them as a student. Each time I had a few minutes between classes, I would sit in the open spaces on the Campus, observing and admiring them because they were mostly women, strong women, who were always up at the crack of dawn to prepare their families for the day, then they would be the first ones on the Campus to set up their stalls daily where they would sell their snacks all day until nightfall, even when it rained. Their realities kept me grounded as a student and I am sure there are other students who feel the same way.

We spent the journey to the airport talking about different bits of our visit and were surprised at how quickly we got there. We joined the check in queue while George returned the van then said our goodbyes to Amanda and my mom when we neared the front of the queue. I hugged and kissed Amanda and when it was my mom's turn it was a more touching affair. As I hugged my mom my eyes brimmed with tears which ran down my cheek and I asked myself, "Where did that come from?" While I was sad about leaving after such a terrific time, it was not like me to be crying in mom's presence like that, the last thing I wanted to do was worry her.

When we released each other I could see the tears falling down mom's cheeks as well which made me feel a bit relieved. I didn't want to think of how much I would miss mom, I closed my eyes tight closing out the thoughts as they bid goodbye to George and the girls. As we entered the check-in desk we waved goodbye to them and they waved back. When we were sitting comfortably on the plane I asked George, "How did your mom and sisters enjoy Jamaica?" He explained that after Althea took charge of them immediately after the wedding she took them on a three-day trip to Montego Bay, Ocho Rios and Negril for sight-seeing, basking, bathing, eating and generally enjoying themselves in a couple of the most popular tourist destinations. For the rest of the time she had them at the shop which gave them a chance to learn about the local culture. "They enjoyed themselves very much Marge," he said. "They wanted to stay a bit longer but unfortunately they had to return to England after only five days." He continued. "Well, they are welcome to come again anytime." I said and he squeezed my hand and gave me a sweet smile before he leaned back on the seat to relax.

BIG SURPRISE

I woke up twisting and turning in George's arms. I was perspiring and felt a bit sick. I thought it might be something that I ate the previous day. I glanced at the clock on my bed side table, it was 0530. "You alright Marge?" George asked with concern in his voice. I didn't want to worry him and I knew he only had half hour left in bed before he would have to get started for the office so I told him it was nothing, just something I ate the day before and as soon as I started thinking of the salt mackerel and dumplings I felt so sick I had to sit up in bed. George jumped up beside me and tried to comfort me but as soon as he started stroking my forehead and telling me everything would be alright I was off the bed in a flash puking my gut out in the toilet. George had followed close behind me into the toilet and was now shielding me with his hands in case I was too weak to carry myself.

When I finally stopped puking I stood up and George held me against him and led me back into bed. He then told me he wanted me to stay in bed until I was completely recovered and I agreed feebly. Then he disappeared downstairs and returned with a large cup of tea. "Marge, drink this, it will make you feel better," he advised and helped me up into a sitting position. As soon as I took a few sips of the tea I was heading for the toilet again with George following close behind me. When we got back to bed he said, "Marge, I have to get you to the doctor." I started by telling him I would try and make an appointment for the next day but he quickly cut in and said. "That won't do Marge, we have to get an ambulance and get you to the hospital now. I'll call off work and make arrangements for the children," he said. I tried to protest but his mind was already made up.

"Marge, it could be food poisoning, now I'm not taking any chances," he continued. I thought about the probability of it being food poisoning and concluded there was a strong possibility. He rang 999 for an emerglency ambulance and they said they would arrive in a few minutes, which he thought was just enough time for us to prepare ourselves.

He then handed me a pair of jeans and a t-shirt and asked me to put them on, then he himself pulled on a pair of jeans and t-shirt and saw me to the car. George was back in the house in a second; he then wrapped the children in blankets and saw them to the back seat of the car. As soon as the ambulance arrives George would see me off without any delay, he would follow behind in the car with the girls, they would all stay with me at the hospital initially but if I needed to stay for a while then George would take the children to stay with his sister, Susan until we could collect them. As I looked out the back of the ambulance glass door at George's black BMW trailing us, I was conscious of how weak and battered I felt, as if I was up all night. I was hoping my condition was not too serious.

"Lord I'm so happy, don't take me yet!" I thought and it hit me how George must be feeling. I felt a bit guilty and angry at myself for being the one to awaken us out of our blissful actuality after we were having such a perfectly happy life together. It was three weeks after our wedding and just under a week since we returned from Jamaica and everything was running very smoothly. George had moved in with us from his small apartment and had taken over paying the bills while we looked for a home together. Now I was sick. I had been so independent for so long.

Already I was a bit uncomfortable about George paying all the bills but it would be even worse if my situation was serious. I had gone back to my usual routine of searching for a job though George had told me repeatedly that he was happy having me stay at home and that he was more than happy to provide for me and the girls but I guess it was just too late to change me. I thought that even if I didn't get to go back out to work for an organization then I could at least look into working for myself at home. I thought that would be a brilliant idea but I would have to think of something, and fast. I suppose I was putting myself through some amount of stress, thinking so hard about finding something to get involved with and at the same time earn an income for myself, tears streamed down my face and I started to shiver.

The ambulance attendant asked me if I was alright and I could feel another bout of puke coming. I had to hold my hand to my mouth. Luckily the attendant saw it coming and handed me a sanitary potty which I had to take firm hold of in ensuring I didn't make a mess all over the transport. "Could it be cancer?" I wondered. I thought about salvation and the churches I had attended, especially the ones I held dear and I wished I had lived my entire life closer to the Lord. I was rushed into the emergency unit at the large Manchester hospital and in no time at all George was at my side with the girls who still had their blankets around them and were now properly snuggled up in the comfortable chairs.

It wasn't long before I was called in to see the doctor and George and the children came in with me. I was so glad I didn't have to be alone at a time like this. I sat facing the doctor and he asked if I was Marjorie Smith and George responded, "Yes, she is," before I could say anything. I was so relieved because I was feeling so weak. George knowingly squeezed my hand and I started to relax and let him deal with things. "I'm her husband and these are our girls," he continued. "We are here because my wife is sick, she has been throwing up everything she has eaten and was awoken by sickness from 0530. We would appreciate it if you could have a look to see what is the cause." "Yes, Mr. Smith, I will have a look into the matter right away," said the doctor. Before the doctor proceeded he announced, "There are just a few questions I have to ask and then I will run some tests." Then without delay he asked, "Mrs. Smith, when was your last period?"

I thought for a minute and expected the answer to just roll off my tongue but this morning I just couldn't believe it! I must not be remembering right! George tried to help but couldn't. "Marge, can you remember?" he asked. I hadn't thought about having my periods nor did I have any need to for several weeks now, with all the demands of the wedding and all. It dawned on me that it had been a while since I had my last period and the reality made me dumbfounded. "Oh my God, I must be dreaming, I couldn't be pregnant?" The doctor seeing my reaction to the question said, "Ok Mrs. Smith, what I'll do is to run a pregnancy test and then we'll see alright?"

He then asked me to pass some urine which I did and in a few minutes he announced, "Well, Mr. and Mrs. Smith, you are about to have your third child. I was numb. Just when I thought my life was perfect and I couldn't get any happier there it was; I was pregnant! George immediately bowed down in front of me where I sat on the chair and said. "Oh my God, Marge, you are pregnant. I am going to be a da da!" He took one breath and then continued, "Marge, you don't know how much I've wanted this. Marge, thank you." I began to cry and he held me in his arms and kissed my tears. "Don't cry sweetheart, everything is going to be wonderful." The girls circled around to hug me while Rosie exclaimed excitedly, "Mom don't cry, it's great! We are getting one more sister!"

We then remembered where we were and realized that the doctor was watching us with a big smile on his face and as he cleared his throat we thanked him happily for his help and left. George took the next couple of days off from work to help around the house since I was sick most of the time and couldn't keep anything down. My mom started advising George on how to prepare certain dishes and teas which would calm and soothe my stomach. Not long afterwards, I found that I was doing much better and George was able to return to work. I was going through some of Melissa's clothes that she had outgrown for a while now and was so happy I never got the chance to throw them out. They were still in good condition; some of them even looked new, now they could serve for the new baby. I was looking less for a job by this time and taking more time out to rest and relax.

One day while watching television, I can't remember the name of the programme now but I remember the host saying, in these times of mass unemployment we have to try and help ourselves. She said we should think of something we are good at, that would also be a reliable source of income, in spite of today's economic climate. I thought to myself, "That's exactly what I've been thinking, so I'm not the only one." I started thinking deeply and soul searching to come up with something I have always been good at. "I've always been good at hair braiding," I thought, "But there might not be much of a market for it where we live and it is very time consuming and extremely tiring, especially given the fact that I am now pregnant." I began to think again and it hit me like a bolt of lightening. "I can't believe I didn't think of it before," I thought. I remembered how good I was at writing short stories at school, so good I was at English Language that I was put in the top English Language class. This was quite a feat because there were seven different English Language classes. Furthermore, I have got so much to tell, it would take at least a couple of books to tell my story.

Later I shared my idea with George and as he collected me in his arms, he said, "Marge, that's a great idea. Not only will you be at home taking care of yourself and the children, you'll be writing books and making an income as well. I'm such a lucky man. I couldn't possibly be happier!" I looked up at him and smiled because I was feeling the same way. I felt sure that I was the luckiest and happiest woman ever. "Oh George," I said. "Thank you for coming into my life and making me so happy, I must be the happiest woman ever." George smiled a sweet, happy smile which melted my heart as he embraced me and I felt at peace in his embrace. After a moment, he pulled his body away from mine and held my head in his sizeable, strong hands as he peered into my soul with big, bright, piercing eyes. "Marge." He said and I waited eagerly to hear what was coming. "You know what I've always thought?" He continued looking ever so serious which made me a bit nervous by this time, wondering what could be wrong. "What?" I enquired in a worried and concerned voice. George swallowed hard as he mustered himself and said in a deep, tender voice, "Marge, I don't know if you feel it too but I always felt we were made for each other." Hot tears ran down my face as I nodded in agreement and George quickly embraced me again in a firm, tight hold and as we stood there in each other's arms, I thought we'd never ever let go.